"We don't know what each ~~much better equipped if we start each day~~ and in prayer. In *Your Next Thirty Days*, my friend Dean Fulks challenges all of us, whether we're new to the faith, returning to the faith, or a seasoned believer. Dean has combined great stories from his own life with timeless principles from God's Word. The result will put you on the path to a closer walk with our Creator."

— *Kevin Ezell*, *President of the North American Mission Board*

"No matter where you are on your journey with Christ, all of us have a next step to take. My good friend, Dean Fulks, has written a powerful new book to help you find your next step to deeper intimacy with God. Enjoy your journey through *Your Next Thirty Days* as you grow in your life-changing relationship with Jesus!"

— *Vance Pitman*, *Senior Pastor of Hope Church in Las Vegas, NV*

"LifePoint Church has baptized hundreds of people and been a frequent guest on the '100 Fastest Growing Churches in America' list. As founding pastor, Dean understands, as few do, what new believers need. *Your Next Thirty Days* is now my answer to, 'What book would you recommend to new Christ-followers?' The network of churches I direct has already placed a huge order."

— *Rich Halcombe*, *Director of MCBA and CEO of Stowe Mission of Central Ohio*

"This book is a must-read! Dean has a powerful ability to open up God's Word and relate it to everyday life with refreshing insights. You will laugh; you will be challenged; you will grow in your faith because of spending time with God through this book."

*– **Sara Gilham**, mom of four and Bible Study Fellowship Teaching Leader*

"Everyone wants to know the secret to success in their spiritual life. Dean's book, *Your Next Thirty Days*, reveals that secret in a new and fresh way that's personal, practical, and powerful. Regardless of where you are on your spiritual journey, I promise this book will move you forward."

*– **Chris Conlee**, Author of LoveWorks: The Key to Making Life Work, Co-Founder and Lead Pastor of Highpoint Church in Memphis, TN*

"My friend and pastor Dean wrote this book on the principles and practice of spending time daily with God. Dean's teaching style makes sense to any who have a desire for that relationship with God or already have one. Whether you're a new believer, have that relationship but need to get back to the basics, or already spend time daily with God and are up for a thirty-day challenge, this book is just for you! Be brave and take a leap of faith! I hope this book challenges you in the next thirty days."

*– **Bryn Smathers**, Christian for two years*

"Dean has been our pastor for several years, and we've been blessed by his ability to take God-sized concepts and break them down into understandable bite-sized pieces. In *Your Next Thirty Days*, you'll be challenged to take next steps in your faith, as you read stories of others who've walked this road and learn practical daily strategies to encourage you along the way. Set aside a few minutes daily for the next thirty days—you'll be changed because you did."

— *Laurie Hise*, *Founder of the passionatepennypincher.com*

"Every major adjustment in our lives must have a beginning. It's like the first few weeks of a diet or working out—if you never start, do not be disappointed in the lack of results! I know and love Dean Fulks and his family. What he teaches in *Your Next Thirty Days* comes from a humble heart and countless hours sitting at God's table learning in order to be fed and disciplined at the same time! What he provides is deep spiritual nourishment to get you started, or maybe restarted, on the path of embracing God's vibrant call for your life! Don't miss it, friend—pick up the book. *Your Next Thirty Days* may be the ticket that will alter the spiritual direction of your next thirty years and more!"

— *Dr. David Wheeler*, *Director of the Center for Ministry Training, Liberty University*

"Dean is one of those rare people who always makes your life better when you are around him. One of the many benefits of his new book is that we don't have to schedule a meeting with him to reap the blessings of his wisdom; we can simply pick up his book. After thirty days of inspiration from his experiences and insights into the Word, we all will have fresh resources for growing in the faith and helping 'elevate' the people we love."

— *John A. Hays*, *Senior Pastor of Jersey Baptist Church in New Albany, OH* get to know Him better personally in relationship. Dean's day by day approach, with practical steps along the way, will definitely make 'your next thirty days' a fulfilling thirty days."

– **Brian Broyles**, *Church Planting Leader and Christian for four years*

"*Your Next Thirty Days* provided the encouragement I needed at exactly the right time. It was a perfect reminder of how valuable it is to spend daily time with my Father, especially when life becomes busy. The results were fruitful and left me feeling spiritually full and loved."

– **Abby Chubb**, *Senior at Olentangy Orange High School*

"In *Your Next Thirty Days*, Dean takes you on a journey into what life looks like when thoughts are synchronized with truth. If applied, this book will change you *and* those around you. How do I know? Because I've watched the author up close, living out these principles over the last ten years. Take it up. Read it in. Live it out. And enjoy what God does in and through you."

– **Brian Frye**, *National Collegiate Strategist, North American Mission Board*

# YOUR NEXT THIRTY DAYS

## DEAN FULKS

**AUTHOR ACADEMY** elite

Published by Author Academy Elite
P.O. Box 43, Powell, OH 43035
www.AuthorAcademyElite.com

Paperback ISBN-13: 978-1-64085-138-2
Hardcover ISBN-13: 978-1-64085-140-5
Ebook: 978-1-64085-143-6

Library of Congress Control Number: 2017914582

Available in hardcover, softcover, e-book, and audiobook.

*To Angie, Sydney, Dillon, and Sylvia for making me a better husband and father.*

*To all of those who are brand-new to Christianity, just returning to God, or looking for a relational life with God — don't settle for normal.*

# CONTENTS

## Part 2 – Hope

## Part 3 – Love

# FOREWORD

As a young boy I loved stories. Turns out Jesus loved stories too—He shared them often with his friends, his followers, and anyone who would listen. One in particular seared my soul—the story of the sower and the seed.

> *Jesus told them many things in parables, saying: "A farmer went out to sow his seed. As he was scattering the seed, some fell along the path, and the birds came and ate it up. Some fell on rocky places, where it did not have much soil. It sprang up quickly, because the soil was shallow. But when the sun came up, the plants were scorched, and they withered because they had no root. Other seed fell among thorns, which grew up and choked the plants. Still other seed fell on good soil, where it produced a crop—a hundred, sixty or thirty times what was sown.*

Naturally a reflective kid, when I heard this story I wondered which of the four "soils" my heart represented. Was I the path, the rocky places, the thorns, or the good soil? I knew one truth for sure; I didn't want the Word of God springing up quickly and then withering due to a poor root system.

Dean Fulks' book—*Your Next Thirty Days*— addresses this phenomenon. Based upon our conversations, I know he isn't satisfied with it either and thankfully he decided to do something about it.

I've had the honor of calling Dean a colleague, then my pastor, and now one of our published authors. After just one chapter you'll realize Dean is a brilliant storyteller. In reading this resource, I know you'll see a man committed to God and his Church.

This book is a tool designed to help us dig deep and combat the tendency of staying shallow. Over a thirty-day period, you'll find yourself growing in your knowledge and application of God's Word. New Christ followers will find the book helpful and those familiar with faith will enjoy its refreshing appeal also.

The concept behind the book is truly unique. As a former pastor of twelve years, I wish I had this resource to hand people. I would have distributed them liberally.

Providentially though, we're all in the business of reaching the lost, whether or not we're pastors. This book removes any apprehension we might feel. After all, each of us can spread the seed of the Gospel confidently, knowing that we have a tool to help people grow in their relationship with Jesus.

I'm excited to see how God is going to use this book to reach a new generation. If we answer the call then just like Jesus promised, it will produce a crop—a hundred, sixty or thirty times what was sown.

Whether you're far from God or you've prayed to Him this morning, prepare yourself for an exciting adventure. You're only thirty days away from a brand new perspective on life. What you discover will reshape the way you see your Creator, your core, and your community.

Welcome to day one!

Kary Oberbrunner, CEO of Author Academy Elite, author of *Elixir Project*, *Day Job To Dream Job*, *The Deeper Path* and *Your Secret Name*

# INTRODUCTION

I never dreamed of planting a church. I never dreamed of multiplying churches. I never dreamed of writing a book. But I always dreamed of making a difference.

This book will NOT change your life. However, it's about a book that CAN change your life. These thirty chapters are about spending relational time with the God who created more than one hundred billion stars (that's actually a septillion, but who's counting?). So, whether you are brand new to following God, you haven't even started yet, or you've been following for years but are looking for a challenge in your devotional life, just give me thirty days. The average person is going to live about 26,000 days. You can do almost anything for thirty of them.

In my late twenties, I was visiting my parents on their small farm in southern Ohio. My dad had a cow that was about to "freshen." ("Freshen" just means the cow is about to have a baby, which is not exactly my idea of "fresh"). Since the heifer in the barn could deliver at any minute, my dad went to check on her before bed. He came back to the house, looked me in the eyes and said, "Get your clothes on; she's having trouble."

At this point, I'm looking around my parents' kitchen and thinking he must be talking to someone else. Maybe he wanted me to go and *pray* for the cow, because I certainly missed calf-delivery class in seminary. It quickly became clear he WAS talking to me, and we were heading to the barn, ready or not. On our way, my dad explained this was the heifer's first calf. He said sometimes the birth canal isn't large enough, so the momma cow might need "help." By help, he meant that we would pull on the calf while she pushed.

When the pickup screeched to a halt, I breathed the cool air and felt a twinge of adrenaline pumping. Were we really going to do what my dad just described?

I walked into the barn, and the momma cow was lying down. Only one hoof was visible from the little calf about to be born. My dad said, "Reach up in there and hold the other hoof while I tie these strings onto the calf."

"Dad," I said, "There are these people called veterinarians. I went to college with one. I could call him."

Not. My. Dad. The Marlboro Man didn't need a vet.

We tied these sea grass strings to that little calf's hooves. The cow would have a contraction, her muscles would tighten, and she'd let out a bawl. And when she bawled, we pulled. This process took thirty minutes. At first, I was looking for hand sanitizer. By the end I was sweaty, dirty and cheering for that mother-to-be. When the calf was finally born, the cow immediately started cleaning it up—the miracle of birth.

Think about it.

The cow was miserable. The calf was uncomfortable. But the brand new life was worth those thirty minutes.

I want to invite you to a thirty-day journey. I hope this path will become a way of life for you. Remember, we can do anything for thirty days, right?

Each day, for the next month, I'd like to give you a principle from the Bible, the book that will change your life. Then, I'll give you an opportunity to practice that principle relationally with God. On day thirty, I will give you a summary of the principles that have been taught to me over a number of years about how to develop a personal relationship with God.

It won't always be comfortable. New life never is. You may be a mom with little kids, a dad with crazy pressure at work, or a student trying to fit in at school. Perhaps you are single, facing tough situations alone. Regardless, we need to connect with our Creator in every season.

Remember, it's thirty days, and in the end, new life is worth the battle.

# DAY 1

## AND ANOTHER THING

Twenty years ago, my brother-in-law was a Music Pastor in a town on the Ohio River. In that role, he directed large church musicals. He once visited a popular Passion Play production (a Passion Play is just a re-enactment of the last week of Jesus's life).

He enjoyed a behind-the-scenes tour and quickly realized the producer wanted the play to seem as realistic as possible. For instance, the Roman soldiers used real swords. That night in the play, when the soldiers came to take Jesus out of the Gethsemane Garden, one of them accidentally stuck one of those real swords an inch into Jesus' real thigh. In the commotion of the scene, the soldiers were able to get Jesus back stage. Someone called 911, and the Messiah was headed to the ER.

The director decided to inform the audience they would be unable to finish the play that night because Jesus was getting stitches. However, one of the Disciples interrupted and volunteered to finish the play in the role of Jesus. He executed the Crucifixion and Resurrection scenes flawlessly. Then came the Ascension. In the Ascension scene, he was attached to a harness under his robe and was literally supposed to disappear from view. At just the right moment, sandbags would be dropped backstage, which would lift Jesus up in the air and out of sight. Remember, the director wanted everything to be realistic.

The new Jesus said, "Lo, I am with you always, even to the end of the age." The stagehands dropped the sandbags, and the Savior dramatically began to rise in the air. However, no one thought to calculate for the twenty-pound weight difference between the old Jesus and the new one. So, Jesus rose up in the air about four feet and, because of his heavier weight, came right back down to the ground. In a moment of acting brilliance, the new Jesus said, "And another thing...."

**2 Timothy 3:16 –** *All Scripture is breathed out by God and profitable for teaching, for reproof, for correction, and for training in righteousness*

One of the most important questions to answer as a believer is whether or not the Bible is sufficient to speak to the greatest needs of our lives. The Scriptures claim they are, indeed, sufficient.

## Day 1 Key Concept: God Still Speaks

Personally, I can't get over the fact that God is still speaking to us. For the rest of our lives, God is saying, "And another thing." He's not giving us new revelation, but He is applying His truth to our lives.

As we begin these thirty days together, about what specific issues in your life do you believe that God is speaking? Take some time to pray and ask God what He wants to you to think, do, or believe. Then, write those in the lines below. Ask God to help you hear Him over the next thirty days.

## I'm New Here

It's not always easy to hear God speak. Author Henry Blackaby says God normally speaks in four ways:

1. Through Prayer
2. Through His Word (The Bible)
3. Through Circumstances
4. Through Other Believers[1]

We'll talk about all four over the next thirty days. As you sense God speaking to you in these ways, write them down in the lines at the end of each chapter.

---------------------------------------

---------------------------------------

---------------------------------------

_____

_____

_____

_____

_____

_____

_____

_____

_____

_____

_____

_____

_____

_____

_____

_____

_____

_____

_____

_____

_____

_____

_____

_____

_____

_____

_____

# DAY 2
## THE GOSPEL IN GOD'S ROOM

When our oldest daughter, Sydney, was four years old (that's four going on twenty-four), I walked into her bedroom and declared as only a dad can, "Honey, I need for you to clean up your room." She quickly responded, "Yes sir, Daddy. Now, can you please get out of my room?"

In that moment, I felt as though I needed to say, "And another thing." So, I asked Sydney to walk into the hallway with me, and pointing to another bedroom door, asked, "Whose room do you think that is?" She said it was her younger brother's room. And I said, "Nope, that room is my room. I just let your brother sleep there. And your room is my room. And this is my hallway; I just let you walk in it. Those stairs? They are my stairs. I just let you climb them. Do we understand each other? Those stairs, this hallway, your brother's room are all mine. And your room…is my room."

Waiting for her to respond to my fatherly insight, I was stunned when my bright, cute little girl looked up at me with her big, hazel eyes and said, "Actually, Daddy, it's God's room." In a moment that only God can orchestrate, I knew she was right. It was as if I was in a theological rap battle with my child. I thought I had laid down truth, but she actually trumped me, dropped the mic and walked off the stage. As it turns out, Sydney pointed out an important principle about our relationship with God.

## Day 2 Key Concept: What's mine is His, and what's His is mine.

As we live each day with God, it's mission critical that we put our whole lives into His hands. That includes our possessions. During my discussion with Sydney, I failed to recognize that God had given me the ability to work, which led to the ability to purchase a home. In my attempt to teach my child a lesson, I was taught a lesson: *being a Christian means everything I have belongs to Him.* Everything I own is to be used for His purposes. But instead of merely taking the word of a four-year-old, let's see how God's Word puts it:

**Psalm 24:1 – *The earth is the LORD'S, and everything in it, the world, and all who live in it (NIV)***

Whether you are brand new to Christianity or a seasoned believer, Psalm 24:1 feels scary. As flawed humans, it's hard to wrap our minds around the reality that my stuff is not MY stuff. It's HIS stuff that He has loaned to me. Why has God given me so much? What's the purpose of my home, my car, and my stuff? God desires us to use everything we own to make much of Him. So, instead of being a stuff-owner for my own enjoyment, I'm a stuff-manager for the glory of God. When we realize our possessions have a purpose, a higher calling than mere personal enjoyment, it makes it a lot easier to see our stuff the way God does and to fully enjoy what He gives to us.

Further, the word "Gospel" means "good news." It's Gospel that Jesus made a path for us to get to God. It's Gospel that we don't have to pay for our own sins. And it's Gospel that our stuff isn't our stuff. Why is it good news that our possessions aren't really ours? Scripture reveals the answer in the book of Hebrews.

**Hebrews 1:2** – *but in these last days he has spoken to us by his Son, whom he appointed the heir of all things, through whom also he created the world*

As Hebrews reveals, God appointed Christ as the heir of all things. Thus, Jesus will "inherit" all of creation from his Father. The Bible also teaches that Christians are "in Christ." So, if Christ is the heir of all things and we are "in Christ," the stunning reality that follows is that we, too, share in Christ's inheritance—eternally. It's a Gospel paradox. We give up control of our stuff now, but as believers we gain a share in everything eternally. It's all God's Room.

As you pray today, think about what possessions, relationships, or even emotions are difficult for you to give up. We need to (literally) give them UP—put everything, especially the stuff that's the hardest, into His hands. Ask God to help you see everything, yes everything, as His. Pray for each specific possession, relationship, or emotion and write down your prayer in the lines below.

## I'm New Here

While giving up control seems scary, it's actually very freeing. The act means you are seeking God's guidance to steer the ship instead of relying on your own ability. Remember, this response won't be automatic. In fact, it will be messy as you try to take this step to honor God with your life and possessions. Still, keep walking, one foot in front of the other, and don't let perfection get in the way of growth.

_____

_____

_____

_____

_____

_____

_____

_____

# DAY 3
## YES, LORD

Everybody needs a person (or persons) who believes the best for you. I have been blessed with such people in my life, and one of them was Clyde Cranford. Clyde lived just over 40 years on this earth believing God's best for people. He mentored me for two hours every week for most of my three years in seminary. He helped me bring what I was learning in the classroom into the "living" room. He focused on application more than information, and his life was a great gift to me. When Clyde left this earth bound for the eternal place he most wanted to go, hundreds of men and women he had mentored stood at his funeral. They were living testimonies of Clyde's faithfulness to God and to his fellow man.

Clyde once told me a story about being invited to a series of meetings at a predominantly African-American church in Memphis when he was a younger man. After the initial singing, the pastor came onto the stage. However, instead of going behind the pulpit, he went straight to the piano and began playing. At first, it was just the sound of the piano keys, but eventually the pastor began singing. He sang only two words, "Yes, Lord." As if on cue, the congregation began swaying and singing with him. Just those two words, "Yes, Lord."

Suddenly, the pastor stopped singing. He walked behind the pulpit and began to pray: "Lord, you've heard our answer. Now, what's the question?" Just like my four-year-old Sydney (who we talked about yesterday), the pastor dropped the mic!

## Day 3 Key Concept: Faith means you say "Yes" before you know.

We all have battles to fight. Sometimes, people will share with me their child's academic or athletic achievements. I pretend to be excited for them, but inside I'm wondering whether or not I should've stressed that more with my children. Then, an acquaintance tells me how he is doing real estate investing on the side to create passive income for his family for future generations. I don't know the difference between APR and NPR, so I feel less than adequate. Even more, at times I sense God saying to me, "And another thing," about a confrontational conversation I need to have but keep delaying. No matter what your personal battle is, a common struggle for a lot of people is saying, "yes," to God when most of us just say, "maybe."

If we can put our "yes" on the table when it comes to our relationship with God, even before we know the question, we can be Christians. Anything less than a "yes" is less than Christianity. Don't be discouraged. It's a growing pursuit, and God, as usual, provides lots of grace.

When a ten-month-old is attempting to walk but falling repeatedly, we don't look at the child and say, "You should just give up. Honestly, kid, you're really bad at walking." In fact, we respond just the opposite! Instead of discouraging them FROM falling, parents encourage their children THROUGH falling. We are, as it happens, excited for the falls. Why? Because falling leads to walking. If you aren't falling, you'll never be walking. Remember, God has this kind of grace for us. He is our Heavenly Father, and He sees us as His beloved children, stumbling as we may be.

> Falling leads to walking

In the end, faith means believing God for a lifetime. Faith is trusting God with our lives, trusting He knows more and better than we do. Today, pray about putting your "yes" on the table. Say "yes" today as a parent, a teacher, a coach, a foreman, or a line worker. You never know. God may want to make a Clyde Cranford out of you.

What specific areas of your life are you sensing the need to say "yes" to God where you've been saying "maybe?" Name them in the lines below. Is there someone with whom you would feel comfortable sharing these areas?

Also is there someone in your life who either doesn't yet know Christ or needs some encouragement? Someone to whom you could become a Clyde Cranford? Take some time this week to pray for and reach out to that individual.

## I'm New Here

We'll talk about this more in these thirty days, but it's important that we are meeting regularly with other believers. Whether it's a small group or class of some sort, God has designed us to encourage each other. Begin praying and looking now for a smaller group of believers with whom you can interact on a consistent basis at a local church.

_____

_____

_____

_____

_____

_____

_____

_____

_____

_____

_____

_____

_____

# DAY 4
## JIM IN THE GYM

Who among us doesn't want to lose ten pounds? Answer: all those folks who say, "I eat and eat and eat, but I just can't gain any weight." Curse you. Most of us have had a front row seat on the workout rollercoaster at some point in our lives. We love the gym; we hate the gym.

I had a great workout group for about five years. At one point, one of the guys (let's call him "Jim") was struggling with attendance. The rest of the group was trying to find ways to help motivate Jim to attend more. By motivation, I mean using seventh-grade-boy sarcasm. One morning, after one of our "motivational speeches," Jim responded, "Hey, if I don't show up tomorrow, Dean, I'll come to your church next Sunday and hear you speak." At first, I thought win-win, right? Either Jim will show up at the gym or he'll be at church. Then it hit me. I realized the source of Jim's bargain. In his mind, "What could be worse than getting up at 5:30 a.m. to workout? What could be so awful that it would motivate me to do something I hate? That's right. Listening to one of Dean's sermons. Yep, that'll do it!"

Sometimes investing in a relationship with God feels more like something we *have* to do rather than something we *want* to do.

## Day 4 Key Concept: Want to > Have to

In life, desire trumps duty every single time. So the question isn't, "what do I have to do?" The bigger question is, "how do I create desire for God and for His Word?" How do we turn something we have to do into something we want to do? The New Testament writer Paul says it this way in his letter to the Philippians:

**Philippians 1:12-14 –** *I want you to know, brothers, that what has happened to me has really served to advance the gospel, so that it has become known throughout the whole imperial guard and to all the rest that my imprisonment is for Christ. And most of the brothers, having become confident in the Lord by my imprisonment, are much more bold to speak the word without fear.*

Writing from prison, Paul reveals that God put him there. God put him in a Roman gulag where he was chained to one of Nero's guards 24-7. These Praetorian guards went on to become Rome's future senators and leaders after they retired.[2] So Caesar Nero, who hated Christians, chained a future leader of Rome to the greatest evangelist the world has ever seen—the apostle Paul! History tells us the Gospel even infiltrated Nero's own home.

By imprisoning him, God did through Paul's circumstances what Paul could have never done on his own—not to mention the fact that Paul wrote a huge portion of the New Testament from that prison. How does that happen? Paul says it happens through the "help" of the Spirit in Philippians 1:19. Now, that's an odd word. "Help" is where we get our word for "choreography". A choreographer is the person who puts together dancers with steps, which creates group movement that becomes a performance. As shown by Paul's time spent in prison, God is the Ultimate Choreographer, placing His people for a movement that becomes the Ultimate Performance—the spreading of the His Name.

> God is the Ultimate Choreographer

Now, think back to the spiritual habits that Christians should regularly engage in: praying, reading God's Word, gathering with other believers in a small group, and worshipping. In those different activities, we do our part. However, as we do, God choreographs those habits within our lives to create desire in us. In other words, as we witness God working in our lives, it pulls us closer and closer to Him.

As believers, we have the opportunity to play a part in God's chorus line of activity in history. So even when people in your family use sarcasm to undermine your faith or when you get bad MRI results from the doctor, Paul reminds us God will choreograph your circumstances into something beautiful as you trust Him. God used Paul's imprisonment to charter the gospel to Rome's highest levels of society; imagine what He can do with your circumstances!

Think about what needs to be rearranged in your life today to enable you to engage in prayer, reading God's Word, connecting with other believers, and serving your community. Write those things down in the lines below.

Pray today that God would help you see how to make these areas a priority for you, so you will be blessed to see His choreography in your life no matter what the circumstances.

## I'm New Here

As you begin to grow in faith, you'll see God's part and your part. Typically, God won't do your part for you. You and I must set aside time to pray, read Scripture, gather with other believers, and reflect. God's part is what we can't do. Only God can weave our part of the story into His bigger narrative of history.

_____

_____

_____

_____

_____

# DAY 5
## SING THE SONG

When I was in seminary, I was involved with a prison ministry for a couple of years. Each week, a small group of believers would go behind bars, have a church service, and meet in small groups with the inmates.

One week I was asked to give the message. I thought it would be a great idea to take my wife Angie (my fiancée at the time), and she could sing prior to the teaching. That particular night, the prison choir sang, so the energy level was through the roof. In front of 150 inmates, Angie stood up to sing.

The prison didn't have instruments, so she had to choose a hymn and sing a cappella. Angie chose "His Eye is on the Sparrow." If you don't know that song, it begins, "Why should I feel discouraged? Why should the shadows come? Why should my heart feel lonely and long for Heaven and home?"

I failed to calculate how these lines from an attractive young lady might hit my incarcerated brothers. Many of them had been locked up in that prison for years. They fought the darkness of discouragement and dreamed about going home. After my wife finished the opening verse, a very large inmate who I didn't know stood to his feet, pointed his finger right at her, and shouted, "Sing the song, Sister! You sing that song!" Angie turned and looked at me sitting behind her on the small platform. I gave her a look that could only be interpreted as, "Please, please keep singing that song."

In the longest recorded sermon of Jesus's ministry, we also find mention of the sparrows when He says:

**Luke 12:6-7** – *Are not five sparrows sold for two pennies? And not one of them is forgotten before God. Why, even the hairs of your head are all numbered. Fear not; you are of more value than many sparrows.*

Jesus reminds us God is the custodian of nature. Nothing escapes His care. That's the divine side of things. From the human perspective, it's not as easy to see. That's the beauty of the song Angie sang to the inmates; nature teaches us that God cares. Like the sparrows, not one of the prisoners was absent from His roll call of care. However, when we wander too far away from God, this is also true:

## Day 5 Key Concept: Fear fogs faith

You and I tend to live with a sense of dread about the "coming shadows." However, Jesus reminds us that God is a sparrow-watcher, and we are far more valuable to Him than sparrows. Nothing against the sparrows, but God set His heart on saving you. He gave His only Son to be a substitute for your sin, so you could become His son or daughter. If God never forgets the fallen sparrow, how much more is He aware of our lives, our pain, and our future?

This is the essence of the Gospel. Even though we are wrecked by sin, we are loved by God. His love hammers sin. As we are transformed by the Gospel, we learn more and more how to trust God. And trust is the antidote to fear. As long as we live in a world that has been stained by sin, fear will exist. But even in the face of fear, we can sing the songs that God gives to us, even in the face of fear, because we trust the Great Sparrow-watcher.

Take a minute to reflect on your greatest fears. Fears about your future, fears about your children, fears about rejection—all of them can paralyze us. Sometimes the circumstantial fears that come to mind are tied to even deeper fears. Write those down below. Pray those fears back towards God, your Heavenly Father. As much as humanly possible, leave them there and sing your song today.

## I'm New Here

As a new believer, it's easy to think, "Salvation is something I've already experienced, so I need to move on to other aspects of faith." However, we need to revisit the Gospel regularly. Contemplate God's love for you as demonstrated through the cross of Jesus. By doing this, your heart and mind will be renewed to God's love, and this will help you grow increasing trust in Him. Remember if God watches all of the sparrows, He's certainly got you in His sights.

_____

_____

_____

_____

_____

_____

_____

_____

_____

_____

_____

_____

_____

_____

_____

_____

_____

_____

_____

# DAY 6
## HOW TO FIGHT THUNDER LIPS

One night it was my turn to choose the movie. So, Angie and I were watching one of the seven greatest films of all time—Rocky, Rocky II, Rocky III—you get the picture. I'm a fan. There's a scene in the third film where Rocky fights Thunder Lips (a.k.a. Hulk Hogan). On screen were these two huge, muscular gladiators. Angie looked at them, looked at me, looked at them again, and said, "I haven't ever really liked big muscles." I tried to discover the compliment hidden underneath the surface, but it was tough to find.

It's fair to say that most folks could roll out of bed cold and walk a mile. However, if I asked you to run a marathon tomorrow, most of us would find a seat on the struggle bus. Maybe you really want to do it. Perhaps you are passionate about the cause the marathon supports. You figure if you put some effort into it that'll be enough to get the job done. Still, effort alone isn't enough. It takes consistent exercise and training. I'll give you a different example.

I grew up in a musical family, and I tried to play a few instruments. Nonetheless, if you want to perform with a professional orchestra, you have to practice numerous hours daily—hours I wasn't willing to invest. I just wanted to play a couple of Lionel Ritchie songs on the piano. But Rocky Balboa wasn't made overnight. The idea of discipline and training is also seen in Scripture. Look at what the Bible says:

**1 Timothy 4:7** – ... *train yourself for godliness.*

No matter how passionate we are, effort will only take us so far. Whether you're developing a mental skill, an athletic ability, or a musical discipline, consistent practice and exercise trump effort every time. We talked on Day Four about how God takes our spiritual exercises (prayer, time spent in His word, fellowship with other believers, worship, etc.) and choreographs them into a growing, deepening belief. Here's our trouble:

## Day 6 Key Concept: We want the product without the process

Instead of transformation, many Christians get caught in the cyclone of behavior modification. Simply put, behavior modification is the idea that if I avoid doing the wrong things, then I am a good Christian.

Unfortunately, behavior modification fails to consider that it is entirely possible to avoid doing all of the wrong things and still not be a "good Christian" or please God. Sometimes, we are just trying to "out-behavior" other people. We subconsciously believe we can leverage God with our good behavior to get Him to do what we want. It's almost as if we think God is lucky to have us. Actually, it's exactly the opposite.

Other times, we're avoiding wrong behaviors out of sheer pride. It's as though we're saying, "Look at what a good Christian I am! Look at me!" This obedience to God isn't a result of love for Him, but it's coming from a love of ourselves. Remember, we are seeking a deepening faith in God—not others' applause.

> We want the product without the process

Over the next twenty-four hours, what spiritual exercises do you need to do? Maybe you need to tell your spiritual story to someone. Maybe you need to go outside of your normal routine to encourage someone. Maybe you could invest some time serving someone else. Name those people and/or those exercises. Then pray, asking for God's help while you execute what's in your heart.

## I'm New Here

Christianity's goal is not that you behave like other Christians. Instead, God wants to shape you to look like Jesus. He works with who you are, not with what you think you should be. In the Bible, Galatians 5 reveals that God wants to produce these attributes inside of us: love, joy, peace, patience, kindness, goodness, faithfulness, gentleness, and self-control. In the end, that's the goal—finding spiritual exercises that are gathered around working with God to produce those qualities in our hearts.

# DAY 7
## WEED EATER THEOLOGY

After we bought our first home, I needed to buy some lawn equipment. One piece I chose was the Ryobi 875 weed eater with a four-stroke engine. The beauty of the four-stroke engine was its ability to operate multiple attachments. You could take the weed eater attachment off and put on the blower attachment, the edger attachment, or lots of others. Just after buying it, I would stand on the driveway daring a leaf or an insect to land there.

One of the struggles for western Christians is treating God like the Sunday attachment. It's easy to fall into a pattern of feeling spiritual on Sunday. However, we just revert to the same person we've always been on Monday and stay that way—until Sunday morning rolls around again. God becomes a Circumstantial Savior of sorts.

In the Bible, Abram—later to be called Abraham—did not see God that way. Who is Abraham? I'm glad you asked. In most large U.S. cities, you can drive by multiple synagogues, mosques and Christian churches within minutes of each other. All of these call Abraham one of their faith's fathers. Understanding spirituality, religion, and intimacy with God are difficult without understanding Abraham. Here is one of the first times the Bible mentions Abraham:

**Genesis 11:31 –** *Terah took Abram his son and Lot the son of Haran, his grandson, and Sarai his daughter-in-law, his son Abram's wife, and they went forth together from Ur of the Chaldeans to go into the land of Canaan, but when they came to Haran, they settled there.*

Genesis says Terah (the leader of their family) took Abraham and Lot towards Canaan—the future Promised Land. However, the family stopped in Haran and *settled* there instead of going on to Canaan. What was the attraction of Haran that steered them off course? Haran's merchant city was loaded with opportunities and distractions. Many times, we "settle" in our own personal Haran. Here's a principle from Abram's life:

## Day 7 Key Concept: God is not a divine accessory

Unfortunately, life's distractions can cause us to treat God as if He's merely an accessory. He becomes our Sunday attachment that we quickly replace on Monday morning. Remember that God is the Sovereign Lord of All. He is the One who determines the plan.

Not. Us.

We don't fit Him into our plan; we fit into His.

Today, in what areas would you say you are trying to get God to accomplish your plan? In what ways have you treated God as though He's an attachment to your life? How can you practically take a step away from settling in your own personal Haran? Write those thoughts and prayers in the lines below.

## I'm New Here

As we are talking about faith in the first week, it's important to note the difference between believing *in* God (i.e. He exists) and believing God (that Who He says He is and what He says in His Word are true). At times, faith means we believe in realities long before we can see them. Remember that trust—praying trust—is the antidote to fear.

_____

_____

_____

_____

_____

_____

_____

_____

# DAY 8
## HEAVEN

So many of us have questions about Heaven. What is it going to be like? Are the streets of gold for real? How about the gates of jewels? Will we know people who've gone there before us? While these are questions from the human perspective, it is interesting to see how differently God speaks about Heaven:

**Hebrews 8:10-11** – *This is the covenant I will establish with the people of Israel after that time, declares the Lord. I will put my laws in their minds and write them on their hearts. I will be their God, and they will be my people. No longer will they teach their neighbor, or say to one another, 'Know the Lord,' because they will all know me, from the least of them to the greatest. (NIV)*

These verses teach us Heaven is more covenants than comforts. In the Old Testament, God

established the old covenant. The ceremonies and
sacrifices performed pointed towards God's new,
future covenant. Hebrews 8 discusses this new covenant where God, through His Holy Spirit, has
written His laws in the hearts and minds of believers.

The Old Testament law, which used to be written
on stone, is now written on the hearts of believers.
This represents a shift from an old, external reality
to a new, internal one. Further, Hebrews reveals,
"they will all know Me." As believers, we "know the
Lord," because His Holy Spirit is within us. Even
more, knowing the Lord also points to the future
reality in Heaven—where we will actually be with
God personally. That means:

## Day 8 Key Concept: Heaven is more about a Person than a Place

Still, there are two questions about Heaven that
bother us more than any others. One of these we are
willing to ask, and the other we are a little afraid to
ask. The question we all ask is, "Am I going?" The
irony is no one really wants to go now, but everyone wants to go eventually. In Scripture, we read
about how a young man once came to Jesus and
asked a very similar question, "What do I have to
do to experience salvation?" Translation: "How can
I be sure I'm going to Heaven?" Jesus answered the
young man the same way He responds to everyone
else—"Follow me." Following Him is THE sign of
security that you are going to Heaven.

As we follow Jesus, it's important to know we are going to stumble a little bit on our faith journey. It's all a part of learning to walk. While following Him, we are going to get "lost" every now and then. However the longer we follow him, the less often we should get lost. And remember, nobody gets lost on purpose.

Interestingly, the young man Jesus talked with had the same thoughts about Heaven as we do—"Just get me to the place!" We want a perfect realm of comfort in the "sweet by and by." However that brings up the question no one really wants to ask aloud: "Is Heaven going to be boring?"

We fear we're just going to be naked, baby angels who play harps all of the time. Will it be boring? The honest answer is, "No and yes," depending on who you are. Remember Hebrews 8 teaches that God's new covenant enables us to "know the Lord." So, for believers, following Christ is about knowing Him. As a matter of fact, that is precisely how the Apostle John describes eternity:

**John 17:3 –** *And this is eternal life, that they know you, the only true God, and Jesus Christ whom you have sent.*

Therefore, for people who actively follow Christ here on earth and know the Lord, Heaven will be an amazing, encouraging journey. The more you know God personally, the more going to Heaven will be like going somewhere you've always wanted to go and yet feel as if you've always been. It will be the most natural next step after life here on Earth.

On the other hand, the more we treat Heaven merely as a place of eternal comfort—as just an escape from the alternative—the less Heaven will make sense. As a matter of fact, if people aren't following Christ personally, why WOULD they choose to go to Heaven? It really doesn't add up for them to look forward to spending all of eternity with Someone they don't already know. Authentic Christianity life is about living the new covenant, knowing the Lord, and preparing your life for eternity.

As we begin to think about eternity, we begin to ponder our legacy. As you pray today contemplate your long-term, spiritual dreams. How do you

> Heaven is more about a Person than a Place

want to be remembered by generations behind you? Write down the characteristics you want to develop and the moments you hope to create before you go to Heaven in the lines below. Then, ask God to help you take steps towards those.

## I'm New Here

As we finish the Faith section of our journey, security becomes an important issue. Sometimes newer believers feel anxious about their decision to follow Christ. "Was it real?" "Why don't I feel the same way I felt right after giving my life to Christ?" Remember, your Christian security is NOT rooted in your ability to feel a certain way. Jesus says those who are His are held in His hand.

Even more, His hands are wrapped by God—the Father's own hand. Nothing…no one can break His grip on us.

_____

_____

_____

_____

_____

_____

_____

_____

_____

_____

_____

_____

_____

_____

_____

_____

_____

_____

_____

_____

_____

# DAY 9
## YOUR EMOJI LIFE

Your emotional life drives how you think. However, if your emotions are your pilot, your plane could be headed for a crash. Thankfully, God wants to help us navigate the ups and downs of our emotional lives. God gave us emotions for good reasons. Passion, for example, stirs our worship. Compassion causes us to want to serve others.

At age four, my family took our first real vacation, and we went to visit my grandmother in Sarasota, Florida. Shortly after arriving, we headed for the beach. While my siblings, parents, and uncle headed into the ocean, I stayed on the shore making a majestic sand castle. After a while, my uncle invited me into the ocean with him. I declined. I had seen commercials for the summer blockbuster of 1975—*Jaws*—and I was no fool.

The tag line on the movie poster for *Jaws* was simple: "Don't go out in the water."

I got the message, even at age four. However my uncle eventually talked me into going out into the ocean—fully sun-screened with a life jacket AND water wings. I loved it! After a few minutes of hanging onto my uncle for dear life, I easily went back and forth a bit from the beach to the ocean. I had been in the ocean with no one else within forty feet of me when I saw it—the shark fin—passing about ten feet away from me. Suddenly I heard the *Jaws* music begin playing in my mind as the shark's dorsal fin disappeared beneath the water.

I couldn't even scream. The only thing I could do was put my water wings in overdrive as I headed to the shore! Just when I thought I was going to make it, the shark surfaced between the shore and me. Water wings in reverse! We've all seen *Shark Week*—the shark opens its mouth, its eyes close, and that double-jointed jaw opens.

The next thing I knew, I woke up in my bed in Florida screaming, "Mom, Mom! There's a shark underneath my covers!" My mom came running into my room during the middle of the night. "Just a dream," she said trying to comfort me. But to me, it was real. I was sweaty, my heart was pounding, and I wanted all of the lights turned on—bright!

My mom was right; it was just a dream. Still, my emotions didn't know it. Later as a young Christian, I learned a valuable principle regarding emotions from author Bob George in *Classic Christianity*:

## Day 9 Key Concept: Our emotions don't know the difference between fact and fiction

Our emotions are just responders to whatever our senses gather. The fact is that while I was in my bed, Jaws was nowhere in my room. However, my emotions didn't understand the facts.

Today we send messages littered with emojis designed to communicate how we feel in the moment. While our emojis may be decent communicators, they are bad leaders. Emotions don't know the difference between reality and romance. They just "digest" whatever we feed our appetites. Our emotions are limited—they can only respond to what our senses take in from the world. Jesus gave us the recipe for handling our emotions:

**John 8:32 –** *and you will know the truth, and the truth will set you free.*

Jesus reveals that truth is the best pilot, the best rudder, the best navigator, and the best captain for your emotions and your heart. As Christ followers, it's critical we understand that the ingredients we consume with our senses (what we see, what we listen to, and so on) create to some degree an emotional cake. That cake may appear appetizing, but we must remember the limits of emotions. In other words, what tastes heavenly isn't necessarily healthy.

We must develop what God calls *discernment*. Discernment is the ability to measure, according to God's truth, what we see, what we hear, and how we feel. Discernment enables us to determine whether what immediately appears good to our emotions is, in fact, good at all. Remember, truth brings freedom.

For example, often the current culture says, "Here's how you handle relationships." As believers we must discern whether or not the culture is correct. Remember the culture's way may be appealing, but how does it hold up against truth? Today, pray about the ingredients in your life. Are you allowing certain messages from the culture to move you away from God? If so, ask God to help you apply His truth and live in freedom.

## I'm New Here

Steering your life in these areas is not easy. Since God is guiding your life, you will begin asking questions about what is best to listen to and watch. Some things may not be "wrong," but they may not be best...for you. There may be things that don't affect you as much as they do others. This is another reason we need to walk with God every day and not rely on our own understanding. We need to hear from God and allow His Word to speak into every area of our lives.

_____

_____

_____

_____

_____

_____

# DAY 10
## BABY FAITH

As we begin talking about Hope over the next nine days, let's define it. Hope isn't a wish or a dream, which is the way we sometimes talk about it in Western culture. Hope is the conviction that someday everything will look as it should instead of how it looks today. Hope is critical to how we see God.

When Angie and I had children, we read a parenting book (by "we" read a book, I mean "she" read a book and told me about it). The book discussed how to discipline your children, regardless of what type of discipline approach a family chooses (timeout, the never-ending countdown, etc.). With our kids (I'm not recommending this for you), we chose to use the form of discipline our parents used—the dreaded wooden spoon.

The parenting book made the following suggestions:

1. Never discipline your children when you are angry (Just like your parents did with you, right?).
2. Constantly talk to your kids using consistent language such as, "That's a good choice" or "You made a bad choice." And speak to them calmly.
3. Consistently go to the same place to execute whatever form of discipline you choose.
4. Always pray when you're finished disciplining your children in order to teach them that God wants reconciliation with them.

Angie and I followed these four steps with Sydney—our first child and a girl—and the steps worked! Parenting success! Then two years later, our son was born.

As our son Dillon grew, we tried to establish the same pattern; we just weren't sure he got it. One day, Dillon grabbed Sydney's favorite doll, named Baby Faith, along with the wooden kitchen spoon with which he had been playing. He looked at the doll and with a cute two-year-old accent said, "Baby Faith, bad choice! Baby Faith, me spank!" Then Dillon headed towards the bathroom, which was our consistent place of discipline. I thought, "Maybe he is getting it!" I watched as he took Baby Faith to the bathroom, sat her on his lap, and proceeded to explain her grievance of the law.

Then to my parenting dismay, Dillon started clobbering poor Baby Faith over the head repeatedly with the wooden spoon. I immediately called Angie to tell her we were raising an ax murderer! After pummeling Baby Faith for a few seconds, Dillon pulled that doll close to his chest and said, "Baby Faith, let's pray."

Some of us see God that way. We imagine that He just sits perched on a divine cloud waiting for us to mess up. Then when we do, God gets out His heavenly wooden spoon to discipline us, and we assume He kind of likes it. However the Scriptures teach us a different view of God and how He sees people:

**Romans 2:4 – Or** *do you presume on the riches of his kindness and forbearance and patience, not knowing that God's kindness is meant to lead you to repentance?*

The Apostle Paul reminds the Romans (and us) that God's heart towards humanity is one of kindness, and His goal isn't discipline. It's repentance. Repentance means we turn our hearts God's direction no matter our circumstances, no matter our failures. We seek God and His way on the best of days and worst of days because we have hope. Hope means that today is NOT forever. Whether today is a mountaintop or a valley...

## Day 10 Key Concept: Hope means your best days are ahead of you

The reason we have hope is we believe God will fulfill His eternal promises, and His kindness steers our hearts to follow Him more. There are days where we don't understand God. There are days when we disagree with God about how situations are working out. Still, hope encourages us that God is big enough to both handle our questions and complaints—all the while working everything into His plan.

Today, pray your questions, your doubts, and your complaints. Maybe things are going well right now. Pray

> Hope means that today is not forever

your gratitude back to Him and specifically name the things that are going well. Confess to Him your need for His presence in your life regardless of your circumstances. He's not holding a wooden spoon. He's not waiting for your failure. He is a perfect Heavenly Father.

## I'm New Here

Part of hoping for God's best for your future means believing God is your good Heavenly Father. For some, this is difficult because your earthly father was not a great model. Remember that whatever you and I dream a father should be, God is an even greater Father than we can possibly imagine.

_____

_____

_____

_____

_____

_____

_____

_____
_____
_____
_____
_____
_____
_____
_____
_____
_____
_____
_____
_____
_____
_____
_____
_____
_____
_____
_____
_____
_____
_____
_____
_____
_____
_____
_____

# DAY 11

## LP

Music has a different language in each generation. From records to cassettes to CDs to digital music, the realm of music is always evolving. Today, we sometimes use the term EP. EP stands for extended play, which is something between a single and a full CD. Typically, an EP is a little too short to be a full CD and a little too long to be a single. On the other hand, a LP refers long play, and it is a vinyl record. Some people romanticize vinyl. However, I distinctly remember my LPs getting scratched when I was a kid. And when you tried to play them, the needle skipped every single scratch.

A big part of living in hope means we focus on a LP life. Life is not a single, but too often, we focus only on what is happening right now. We forget that we will live eternally, and what happens today is part of a longer journey. Here's another way to say that:

## Day 11 Key Concept: What happens IN you is more important than what happens TO you

Your destination is more important than your today. Now, the obvious difficulty is that how you respond to God today determines your path. And that path ultimately determines your destination. Think LP. What is your vision for the end of your life? What if you thought of yourself more as a farmer and less as a stockbroker?

Stockbrokers have to respond to the ups and downs of the market minute by minute. Farmers, however, do only what they can do. They plant seeds, hoe weeds, pray for rain, and wait for the harvest. Farmers cannot make seeds grow. Farmers cannot control the weather. Still, they can create an environment that hopefully leads to growth, and growth takes time and patience.

My wife's grandfather, Gray Allison, is an excellent example of living the LP life. When he was barely twenty years old, Gray flew a crew of ten men on a B-24 bomber in World War II. After coming home from the war, he married, started a family, graduated from seminary, and even wrote a short book on Jude, one of the last books in the Bible. There aren't a lot of books written about Jude.

In 1969, Gray and his wife went on a mission trip to Southeast Asia. While there, they hopped a small plane over to South Vietnam. As he was visiting a mission in Da Nang, Gray noticed an Army hospital. As a veteran, he was allowed to visit wounded soldiers. So, he began going bed-by-bed, meeting wounded soldiers, hearing their stories, and praying with them.

As he approached one bed, the injured soldier looked up at him, and Gray introduced himself: "I'm Gray Allison. I served in WWII…." Lying on his cot, the injured soldier interrupted him, "Did you say your name was Gray Allison?" "Yes," he responded. The soldier followed up, "Did you write a little book on Jude?" "Well, yes, I did," Gray said. "Somebody gave me your book. I read it. I became a Christian reading that book."

I have learned a lot from Dr. Gray Allison. He loves his family. He has given the weight of his life towards influencing the world to Christ. He plays the long game…always living LP. While today's life can feel a bit like a rollercoaster, we still must live with a vision for eternity. Living LP gives us hope, a concept that resounds throughout the Scriptures:

**Romans 5:4-5** – *and endurance produces character, and character produces hope, and hope does not put us to shame, because God's love has been poured out into our hearts through the Holy Spirit who has been given to us.*

As the Apostle Paul reveals in Romans, one of God's designs for our LP life is that through life's struggles we will endure. And endurance ultimately produces hope in us. Thus, what is happening outside of us is affecting what is developing inside of us. So, what happens *in* you is more important than what happens *to* you.

Take a few minutes right now and write in the lines below. Describe your vision for your life ten years from now, twenty years from now. How do you want your relationship with God to look? How about your marriage? Your relationship with your kids? Then, begin praying those things, planting those seeds, and making a difference in the LP.

## I'm New Here

Some people become Christians during a time of crisis. God can use any situation to draw us to Himself. At the same time, it's important to remember that becoming a Christian does not mean your situations and circumstances will always improve. We come to God through Christ because we respond to His love for us on the Cross—not because we get a better life.

_____

_____

_____

_____

_____

_____

_____

_____

_____

# DAY 12

## ONE WHALE OF A STORY

Jonah is a confusing story in the Old Testament for many people. Some say, "How could a guy get swallowed by a huge fish for three days and still live to tell about it?" However, if you believe God created the world, then it follows that doing a miracle every now and then is really no big deal for God. I would suggest that Jonah's experience was a signpost for us.

When Angie and I had been married five years, I was blessed to have my way paid to a conference in Hawaii. Thus, we gathered every spare dollar we could find and managed to buy Angie a ticket to go with me for our 5th anniversary. I wanted to go... go...go. Angie, however, had been going...going... going...chasing around little kids, so she didn't quite share my enthusiasm. So, we compromised and did what I wanted to do (hopefully, I've gotten a little wiser in the last sixteen years).

In Hawaii, we went touring and snorkeling; it was amazing! I also wanted to see whales and found a local company that had two tours in the morning. Tourists received a discount for the early morning tour, so guess which one I chose? There we were, 7:30 a.m. in the morning, on the deck of this seafaring boat with only three other customers. The crew readied the boat, and soon we pulled out of the Honolulu harbor and drove about thirty minutes. Finally, the captain stopped the boat and sent us all, customers and crew, to the edges of the boat to look for the "kahola," which is Hawaiian for "whale."

After a few minutes, someone spotted one. But at about four hundred yards away, we barely could see the whale surface. To my excitement, the captain started the boat and headed in the direction of the whale. But to my dismay, he only took us about one hundred yards before stopping. At that time, international fishing laws would only allow us to get within one hundred yards of a possible whale. In my mind, I had envisioned our boat chasing them down. But for the next hour, we'd see a whale that was a few hundred yards away, drive the boat kind of that direction, and hope they'd come closer to us. They didn't.

Finally, the captain said it was time to head back to the mainland. Mentally, I was taking inventory. I had just spent money we probably didn't have to see whales that were barely visible; I had to save this experience. On the way back to shore, I asked the captain if Angie and I could walk out to the bow of the boat. I had Angie spread her arms out, and I sang the *Titanic* song; she was not amused.

On the way to shore, I randomly asked the captain if I could drive the boat. He looked oddly for a minute and then said, "Okay." In the background, it seemed as though you could hear the *Gilligan's Island* music playing, "The Minnow would be lost." Suddenly, with me driving, a massive, blue whale surfaced right in front of our boat. The captain grabbed the throttle and threw it into reverse, and I turned the wheel. I couldn't believe it!

Our boat snuggled up right next to a huge, blue whale. The crew screamed, "Kahola, kahola!" The whale was so close to our boat, it felt as if you could reach out and touch it. Suddenly, the whale submerged, and its calf surfaced, smacking its smaller tail and getting us all wet. For what seemed like hours, nobody said a word as a group of whales swarmed around our boat, performing what seemed like an orchestrated, oceanographic ballet. Eventually, the school moved into other waters.

Now, I have seen whales at Sea World doing tricks for sardines. However, when you see them, all 300,000 pounds of them, in their natural element, they are captivating. A blue whale's tongue weighs as much as an adult elephant, and their length measures three school buses! When I saw these wild creatures, untamed and powerful, I knew they could've sunk our boat at any minute. There is no comparing the whales on display at a park with the whales in the wild.

Many people want a god they can ask to do Sea World tricks for them, a god they can manipulate. However, those folks are sorely disappointed in authentic Christianity. Unfortunately, many land on that kind of "Sea World trick" religion, but that's not the God of the Bible.

Earlier, I called Jonah a signpost for us because that's what Jesus said:

**Matthew 12:38-40 –** *Then some of the scribes and Pharisees answered him, saying, "Teacher, we wish to see a sign from you." But he answered them, "An evil and adulterous generation seeks for a sign, but no sign will be given to it except the sign of the prophet Jonah. For just as Jonah was three days and three nights in the belly of the great fish, so will the Son of Man be three days and three nights in the heart of the earth.*

Jesus's listeners said, "Give us a sign." In other words, "Do a trick for us; entertain us." What was Jesus's response? "You will only get the sign of Jonah, who spent three days and nights in a whale, and so shall the Son on Man be." In short, Jesus revealed how Jonah's story was meant to point us to Him. Just as Jonah spent three days in a whale, Jesus spent three days in the belly of the earth after being crucified. Yet on the third day, God raised Jesus from the dead.

This is the Gospel of Easter—"but now Christ is raised from the dead," as Paul says in the New Testament. If there's no Easter, then there's no hope of Heaven, which means no end to sin, pain, and suffering. Without the hope of heaven, there's no long-awaited reunion with the people you love or ultimate healing from disease.

On the other hand, if Easter is a real event that occurred, then that changes everything.

What this means for us is, no matter what our circumstances are, we have hope. If you are going through the tough middle school years, there's hope. If you're in college or just out of college and trying to make ends meet financially, there's hope. If your marriage feels like one long fight, there's hope. If you're a single parent (perhaps the toughest job in the world), there's hope.

In that same chapter, Paul says, "Oh grave where is your victory...oh death, where is your sting?" The Message Bible says it this way: "Who got the last word, Death...who is afraid of you now?" That's Paul trash-talking death!

Today, the only thing that's left for you is to appropriate this hope to your life, to your soul... today. You and I don't need a miracle as much as we need a Savior. Remember:

## Day 12 Key Concept: God wants a relationship with you more than a religion for you

As you pray today, think about the ways you settle for religion in place of a relationship with God. Ask God to show how you have simply imitated what you've seen others do. Maybe you think church attendance makes you spiritual, so you show up but only go through the motions. Maybe you follow rules you think other spiritual people follow, but you don't know why. Perhaps you just think God is keeping score, so you want to make sure you are winning.

## I'm New Here

One snag Christians regularly encounter is trying to get God to accomplish their plan as opposed to joining God's already existing plan. Remember, God has a plan, and we get to be part of it. The most exciting steps in the Christian journey are watching God do what only He can, instead of settling for a Sea World version of god.

_____

_____

_____

_____

_____

_____

_____

_____

_____

_____

_____

_____

_____

_____

_____

_____

_____

# DAY 13

## HARD WORK

One of the unique realities for westerners is that we work—A LOT. Americans, for example, are the most overworked country in the Industrialized World. Eighty-six percent of American workers put in more than forty hours per week. Annually, we work 137 hours more than Japanese workers, 260 hours more than Brits, and 500 hours more than French workers.[3] Regardless of what you think about that—right or wrong, left or right politically—what do those numbers tell us? Our hearts need to be rearranged regarding work.

### Day 13 Key Concept: Instead of working to live, we are living to work

There was a popular song in the 1980s about work called, "Take This Job & Shove It."

We love work; we hate work.

However, the reality is we are, in fact, created to work. Cultivating the ground was part of Adam's role before sin entered into the world in Genesis 3. The Bible describes over two hundred different occupations. In all of the Old Testament, it's interesting that only one person is said to be filled with the Holy Spirit, and it wasn't Moses, Abraham, or King David.

**Exodus 31:2-5** – *"See, I have called by name Bezalel the son of Uri, son of Hur, of the tribe of Judah, and I have filled him with the Spirit of God, with ability and intelligence, with knowledge and all craftsmanship, to devise artistic designs, to work in gold, silver, and bronze, in cutting stones for setting, and in carving wood, to work in every craft."*

Clearly, God gifted Bezalel with many abilities and talents for the purpose of work. Still, we need balance. We cannot worship work because work makes a really bad god. God's applause must be primary to any other applause, including that which comes from your boss or your work peers.

Paul gives us the other end of the spectrum concerning work in the book of Colossians.

He says that some just work by way of "eye-service." This kind of labor—where we only work hard when the boss is watching—is performing for eye-service. My dad called that "lazy man's work." You are trying to get paid more than you actually work, since you don't see your work as a reflection of your heart and character. In this situation, work actually isn't important enough in your life.

So, what's the correct view of work? God has placed you in your current job for impact, not just income. As a Christian, your primary work is to use

> **Work makes a really bad god**

your talents, gifts, and abilities to make a difference in others' lives and not just in your own life.

Jesus did not die for us to have a wrinkle-free life. Remember, ownership is a myth, but stewardship is a reality. Once Jesus told a story about a very rich guy who took a trip and left his money with his servants. The owner asked the servants to invest the money (in the story, the money is called "talents"), so that the talents earned interest while the owner was away.

The three servants received five, three, and one talent(s) respectively. The servants who received five and three talents invested them, as asked by the owner. But one servant didn't invest his single talent as asked. When the owner came home, he was furious with this disobedient servant. The owner took the one talent away from him, gave it to one of the others, and punished the servant.

That always sounded kind of severe to me. At least the third servant saved the money, right? What's so bad about what the servant did? Here's the rest of the story. A talent was worth 10,000 denarii in their world. To put it in perspective, one denarius was an average day's wage. So, if you figure 250 working days per year, then you are looking at forty years of work represented in each talent. So, the servants received five talents (or five lifetimes sums of money), three lifetime sums, and one lifetime sum.

Now, do you see the point? Put a dollar figure on what God has done for you. How many lifetime sums is that worth? The point of the parable is that you and I aren't owners; we are stewards who've been given *more* than five lifetimes sums of money—we've been given eternity. So, we invest what we've been given down here for eternal rewards up there.

Today, pray about your work. You may work a full-time job outside of your home. Perhaps you work as a stay-at-home mom. Maybe you are a student, so your education is your work. Are there areas where you've allowed work to become god in your life? If so, confess those. Pray that God would occupy the highest place in your life. Are there areas where you are doing as little as possible? God has gifted you with talents and abilities to make a difference. Pray through those areas as well.

## I'm New Here

In the West, we spend a huge part our lives at work. Whether you love the actual work or you don't, see your workplace as a mission field. God has placed you in that job (as much as it doesn't contradict His principles) for an impact on people and not just income. Begin praying regularly for your co-workers and for how you can be part of planting spiritual seeds in their lives. Trust the Bible for your questions about work. The Bible is like Home Depot for spiritual principles about work. It has everything you could ever need.

_____

_____

_____

_____

_____

_____

_____

_____

_____

_____

_____

_____

_____

_____

_____

_____

_____

_____

_____

_____

_____

_____

_____

_____

_____

_____

_____

_____

# DAY 14

## THE ALMIGHTY MAKER OF HEAVEN AND EARTH

Throughout Christian history, groups of believers wrote creeds, which are simply statements of belief. Maybe the most famous of these is the Apostles Creed, which is still quoted regularly in many churches. The first line reads, "I believe in God, the Father Almighty, Maker of heaven and earth, and in Jesus Christ, his only Son, our Lord." This statement flows from the beginning of the book of Genesis:

**Genesis 1:1 –** *In the beginning, God created the heavens and the earth.*

Interestingly, when Genesis says, "God created," the word used for "created" is the word "bara." This word is used about fifty times in Scripture and only about God's creating work. Even more, in forty-nine of those fifty uses, "bara" is used to describe God creating parts of the natural world. The only other time "bara" is used occurs in Psalm 51:

**Psalm 51:10 –** *Create in me a pure heart, O God…*

The link between creation and us is pretty clear. Only God could create the natural world, so it follows that only God can create a new heart in us.

Today, we have a lot of questions about the *method* of creation. However, the *meaning of* creation is just as, if not more, important. We see it from the earliest stories in Genesis including the story of the first siblings, Cain and Abel.

Both brothers brought an offering to God but with very different results. Cain brought an offering of produce, and Abel brought the firstborn of his flock. Abel's offering was regarded favorably by God, but Cain's was not. Why did God value Abel's offering more than Cain's offering? Cain brought some of his produce in response to the harvest, but he had more harvest at home. Abel offered his only firstborn lamb.

For Abel, this was an all or nothing premise. By offering his firstborn lamb, Abel was not guaranteed he would have another. Abel trusted that God would provide for his future, so his offering was an expression of faith. However, even after this incident, God's specifically expresses His love for Cain in Genesis 4.

**Genesis 4:6-7** – *The Lord said to Cain, "Why are you angry, and why has your face fallen? If you do well, will you not be accepted? And if you do not do well, sin is crouching at the door. Its desire is contrary to you, but you must rule over it."*

God shares an important principle with Cain:

## Day 14 Key Concept: Either you rule your produce or your produce rules you

It seems as though Cain wanted to give God the absolute minimum. When I was in college, I lived with five other guys, and we had some simple rules in our apartment. We tried to abide by the Law of Discovery—if you discover it, you deal with it. One of our constant frustrations was toilet paper. The idea was that if you finish off a roll of toilet paper, you put a new one in its place. However, it seems there was a loophole in the law. Consistently, someone would come to our apartment, walk into the restroom, and find one half-sheet of toilet paper hanging on for dear life from the cardboard roll. In life, you can be "technically" right and still be wrong.

Shortly after God's conversation with him, Cain murders his brother Abel. As always, God was right. God had warned Cain that his produce ruled his heart. As a result, Cain lacked the capacity to deal with jealousy. Jealously controlled him, and he became a killer.

However, there are other times in life when people respond to disappointment in rare, beautiful ways that we cannot explain.

A young couple from our church, Josh and Steph, had been trying for some time to become pregnant with their first child. There were ups and downs throughout the process, but finally Steph was expecting. Not far into the pregnancy, they received the news that no parent-to-be wants to hear. Their doctors told them their baby had developed Thanatophoric Dysplasia, a rare skeletal disorder that affects about 1 in 60,000 births and, sadly, is almost always fatal. For Josh and Steph, this meant their sweet child might not survive long after delivery. So, while they were preparing for a birth, Josh and Steph were simultaneously preparing for a funeral. I had the opportunity to pray with and for them.

When the day arrived for their son Noah to be born, Josh and Steph headed to the hospital. On the way, they listened to worship music and prayed over the baby. After Noah was born, he was rushed to the NICU where the doctors examined his condition. It was there in the NICU that Josh and Steph received the news that crushed their hope—the doctors determined little Noah was not going to survive. They rushed Noah back to Steph, so the family could all be together for the little time they had left.

While Noah had been examined in the NICU, he had been away from his mother Steph for over an hour. Steph, who had kept a journal about the entire experience, explained her frame of mind as she waited for her son:

*For the first time, my hope was shattered and all I could feel was pain and anger. My worst nightmare was becoming reality and it was happening too fast for me to comprehend. I was so afraid that if my time with him (their son Noah) was short, I would be too emotional to really be with him. When they walked in the room and handed him to me my heart changed. I was so happy to finally hold my son, and I felt so much peace and joy in that moment. Of course, I was still devastated knowing I would soon lose this precious little life, but I was given a strength that was not my own. God was in control and even though He was not answering my prayers the way I wanted Him to, He was faithful in His promise.*

She posted the promise from Scripture:

**Philippians 4:6-7 –** *"do not be anxious about anything, but in everything by prayer and supplication with thanksgiving let your request be made known to God. And the peace of God, which surpasses all understanding, will guard your hearts and your minds in Christ Jesus."*

God did something for Josh and Steph that we cannot do. He renewed them with a supernatural strength that was not their own. It's the reality that God is THE Creator, capable of making things above and beyond our wildest imaginings. If He can create the world, then He can create the kind of strength and peace that sustains parents who are losing a son.

In the Bible, the Almighty Maker of Heaven and Earth says, "*Behold, I am making all things new!*" As you pray today, pray about the *produce* of your life. Maybe that's a bonus at work or the accumulation of your financial resources. Maybe that's your ability as a mom to raise successful kids or cook really great dinners. It could be your report card or your stat sheet after a big game. Either you lead those things or they lead you. Pray that God would do what only He can do – create a clean heart in you as you pursue Him.

## I'm New Here

Dealing with disappointment, as Cain did, has the potential to temporarily derail our faith. Sometimes, we get our way because our way is best. Sometimes, God saves us from the consequences of our way. As a perfect heavenly Father, He knows better than we do. Other times, we are persistent children who want our own way, and God gives it to us—along with the consequences. In the end, even after Cain murdered Abel, God still gave him grace. He offers that same grace to us in our failures as well. So don't give Him the absolute minimum—give God your best.

_____

_____

_____

_____

# DAY 15
## THE BEST REST

One Christmas, when our kids were eight, six, and three, we spent six days with my wife's family to celebrate the holiday. On the seventh day, we drove home; I always thought the seventh day was a day of rest. The kids were in the back of the van, and I had been driving for about five hours. For almost an hour, my wife drifted so peacefully off to sleep in her passenger seat. It wasn't just any sleep. I am talking about mouth-open, drool-on-your-collar sleep.

I was a little jealous of her Rip Van Winkle catnap. Okay, I was A LOT jealous—and bitter. Somehow, I came up with the bright idea to have her drive after she awoke from her hibernation, so I would have the same opportunity to rest. The switch worked perfectly…at least in the front of the van.

In the back of the van, things suddenly changed. Our eight-year-old had received a portable cd player for Christmas. She began singing *High School Musical* songs sans music for the rest of us, so we could only hear her vocals. My son wanted food and then drinks and then candy. He just kept saying my name, "Dad...Dad...Dad," which is Hebrew for, "Your job is to give me whatever I want." All the while, our youngest child just kept yelling, "No!"

I quickly realized that I no longer wanted the passenger seat job. My wife and I switched back places.

Still, the noise continued. One was singing off-key vocals, one had the munchies, and one was yelling at the top of her lungs. It reminded me of going to a Van Halen concert. I don't know exactly what happened to me, but suddenly I exited the highway at Carrollton, Kentucky—FOUR hours away from our home.

This is what came out of my mouth: "Kids, you will all be living in Carrollton, Kentucky for the rest of your lives, right here at this Shell Gas station! They have plenty of good food and a bathroom. You'll start at Carrollton Elementary School next week. Mom and I will bring you presents next Christmas." As our stressful journey home revealed, nobody enjoys trips that last longer than they should.

The people of Israel went on a trip of sorts. It also lasted longer than expected, about forty years longer than expected. The Israelites wandered in the wilderness for four decades, walking in circles and facing all kinds of peril. At times, they chose the wilderness over trusting God to take them to the Promised Land. All the while, they constantly complained. Let's look what the book of Hebrews has to say about it:

**Hebrews 3:18-19** – *And when he swore that they'd never get where they were going, wasn't he talking to the ones who turned a deaf ear? They never got there because they never listened, never believed. (MSG)*

As the book of Hebrews shows, the Israelites' problem wasn't the wilderness. The failure of the Israelites was that they didn't listen and they didn't believe. We have the same struggle.

## Day 15 Key Concept: Our problem is our will, not our wilderness

Just like the Israelites, you and I battle to listen and believe. Trusting God is easy to talk, yet difficult to walk. That's why spending part of your day —each day—listening to God through His Word is so critical. That's how we will find rest.

Rest is also mentioned during Creation. When God created the world, He rested on the seventh day. Unlike us, He did not rest because He was tired. He's not subject to a fallen, physical body as we are. He rested FOR us. He rested to show us something; He rested to teach us something.

> Our problem is our will, not our wilderness

Jesus made a comment in John 5: "My Father is always at work." What does it mean then if God, who is always at work, rested? I think it means that on day six of Creation, God stopped creating and started reigning. The seventh day was the inauguration of the Kingdom of God in this world. On that day, the King took the throne.

After you drive the last nail into a home you have built, you spend your first night there. You eat your first family meal there. You aren't working on it; you are reigning in it.

Ever since Adam and Eve sinned, we have been working hard, seemingly without rest. That is part of the curse. However, we have not just been working physically, we also work spiritually. There's something inside of us that thinks we can be good enough for God, so we are never resting. We are always trying to prove ourselves—prove we're good enough.

John Gerstner is said to have commented on the writings of Jonathan Edwards this way, *"The main thing between you and God is not so much your sins; it's your damnable good works."* So as believers, how do we rest here on Earth? The book of Hebrews explains the answer:

**Hebrews 4:8-11 –** *For if Joshua had given them rest, God would not have spoken of another day later on. So then, there remains a Sabbath rest for the people of God, for whoever has entered God's rest has also rested from his works as God did from His. Let us therefore strive to enter that rest, so that no one may fall by the same sort of disobedience.*

The writer of Hebrews reveals there is another rest for Christians—a spiritual rest. So, the Sabbath teaches us that Jesus is our Substitute. Jesus' work takes the place of our work. As a result, you must rest from your work of trying to be good enough for

God; you don't have to prove yourself. As a matter of fact, you cannot prove yourself.

Hebrews 4 teaches us why Jesus came. Right before He died, when Jesus was on the Cross, what did He say? "It is finished." When Jesus said those words, the price of your sin was paid. Now, you and I can have real rest as we believe the truth that the only Person from whom we need approval is the One who has already given it to us through His Son.

This means you do not have to live for anyone else's approval. As a matter of fact, you cannot live for anyone else's approval. At least, you cannot live for anyone else's approval and have rest. God did not have His Son die on a cross so that we could have a nice career. Jesus did not sacrifice Himself, so you could date just the right person. Jesus didn't brutally die, so we would spend the majority of our time discovering more comforts.

More important than your physical comfort is knowing that on your worst day, in your worst wilderness, God is never leaving you. He won't drop you off in Carrollton, Kentucky. He never gives up, even when we do. Each day, in the middle of doubt and failure, we can go to Him. So live *from* His approval, not *for* His approval. Jesus already gave it to us.

As you pray today, what are the barriers that keep you from resting? To whom are you constantly trying to prove yourself? Remember, you are asking them to do for you what only God can. Pray today that you would personally recognize that God alone has first place in your life.

## I'm New Here

The fact that God provided us rest in the person of Jesus means the end of people pleasing. Unfortunately, we work very hard in this life to impress others. The Scriptures are clear that we are to be kind and care for others, but we cannot live for others. We live from our relationship with God. He alone is our reservoir to make a difference in others' lives.

# DAY 16

## THE HUMAN RACE

I have been taught my whole life that racism is wrong. Bigotry, prejudice, and marginalization do not have a place in our world. I grew up singing this little song in church, "Jesus Loves the Little Children." The most memorable line from the song says, "Red and yellow, black and white, they are precious in His sight. Jesus loves the little children of the world." Yet, racism exists. Most people would agree *that* racism is wrong, but maybe those same people would not agree *why* it's wrong.

Even the Declaration of Independence declares that all men (and women) are "created equal," but why? America's Founding Fathers wrote that for a simple reason. In the Bible, Genesis 1:27 teaches all people are created in the image of God.

But two chapters later in Genesis, the problem of racism surfaces. Adam and Eve sinned, and as later revealed in Romans 5, through one man's (Adam's) sin, sin was passed down to all men. So, what was once a harmonious world became a sin-filled world. Because of sin, humanity would be filled with strife and human relationships would be plagued by sin.

It's been said, "Racism is a sin problem not just a skin problem."

One conclusion from the Scriptures is that if all men and women fall prey to sin, then they all need the same Savior. By sharing the same Savior, they become part of the same family—all leading to the same Heaven. So, *same* image of God...*same* sin...*same* need...*same* Savior...*same* family...*same* Heaven...do you see a pattern?

In the Old Testament, the Jewish Temple had certain areas that allowed only certain people to enter. During that time, Gentiles could only go to a certain space and then there was a wall. Women could only go to a certain space, and they ran into a wall. Hebrew men could go so far before they, too, ran into a wall. In the Temple, there was discrimination. Thousands of years ago, God was building this idea:

Sin builds walls of separation.

In our world, the walls look a little different: men versus women, black versus white, rich versus poor, Democrats versus Republicans, young versus old, urban versus rural, and people who think the Cleveland Browns are going to the Super Bowl versus normal people. Okay, so the odds say that someday even the Browns will be crowned NFL champions—right before Jesus returns.

We are all separated by sins such as anxiety, anger, violence, insecurity, self-pity, arrogance, hoarding, and pride. However, the Scriptures reveal that there is a remedy for sin; there is a way to tear down the walls that divide us.

We won't do it perfectly. We are going to make mistakes sometimes. At times, we feel as if no one is trying. Sometimes, we will try too hard.

I'll give you an example...shopping. Sometimes I see things on the rack that someone my age shouldn't try to wear. I remember buying what I thought were amazing jeans with the American flag sewn into the back pockets. Every time I wore them to church, my friends would stop and salute as I walked by them. We are not always going to get it right.

**Ephesians 2:14 –** *For He himself is our peace, who has made us both one and has broken down in his flesh the dividing wall of hostility*

As Ephesians 2 teaches, Jesus came along and broke the walls of separation. To say it another way:

## Day 16 Key Concept: Jesus brought unity, not uniformity

If anyone ever knew what it was like to be falsely accused because He was a threat to the establishment, Jesus knew. If anyone ever knew what it was like to be lobbied by groups of people only to be used to meet their selfish ends, Jesus knew. If anyone ever knew what it was like to suffer unjustly for something you never did, Jesus knew. If anyone ever showed us how to deal with issues regarding race, it was Jesus.

Through the Cross, Jesus brings a multicultural healing that reveals more of God's glory. Now, I do not claim to know the practical steps to heal all of the complex issues of regarding race. However, as you pray today, think through your life practically. Are you a wall-maker or a wall-breaker? Do you have the tendency to segregate people based on their income, their culture, or their gender? The Gospel reveals that we are ALL flawed, which destroys superiority. There's no room for one person to think he or she is better than anyone else. At the same time, we are incredibly loved by Jesus through the Cross, so there's no room for individuals to think they are inferior to anyone else either. Pray both of these directions today.

## I'm New Here

Jesus brings us together in unity even though we come from different places and express different cultures. This is critical in our understanding of both salvation and our beliefs about eternity. Heaven will not be segregated. The unity we see in the book of Revelation is every tribe, every tongue, and people from every nation gathered together for eternity. We should embrace that kind of attitude about our differences today.

# DAY 17

## THE PAIN WITH PAIN

When a tragedy occurs, pain is ever-present. In addition to the pain of *what* actually happens, there's the pain of *why* it happens. We have questions—lots of questions. As a matter of fact, we are long on questions and short on answers. Periodically, tsunamis, hurricanes, and earthquakes have devastating effects.

Same questions and same non-answers.

While we don't have all of the answers, we do see some similarities. First, there seem to be two common categories of answers. We will call one category "religious." The religious answer is something like, "If you live a good life, you will have a good life." The problem with this answer is you cannot make it past the story of Job with that perspective. Let's call the second answer category "rebellious." This answer sounds something like, "Because there's an inequitable distribution of pain, God is either mean or He is not in control." Both ideas seem to contradict the nature of God.

While the Scriptures are incredibly helpful in our lives, most of us still struggle to some degree with the "why" questions. Here's my pastoral confession: I feel as though I should have an answer for those going through tragedies, but I don't. The truth is I don't know why, and neither does any other human being. However, the next best thing may be looking into the Bible for some observations about tragedies.

In Luke 13, Jesus brings up a local tragedy. A tower in Jerusalem had fallen, the tower of Siloam, and eighteen people were killed. When someone asked Jesus the "why" question, He didn't shy away from the answer. If I were to paraphrase His response, it would be:

**"This happened, so repent."**

The problem with the religious answer of "living well leads to a good life" is that I don't see my own imperfections. The underlying assumption of this perspective is that "we" are *good* people. But in reality, we are all broken and flawed. On the other hand, the mistake in the rebellious thinking is that we can't seem to make it past the immediate pain. So, we lose sight of God's perfect love demonstrated by sending His only Son to die in our place.

One great attribute of God is that He is always constant in His love. What a reassuring concept! As humans, we find such comfort in His consistency. For example, no matter where you go, McDonald's menus are the same. You can get a Big Mac in Maine,

Mexico City, or Madrid. God's care for you is like that even when you may not feel it.

All of that leaves us questioning again. If neither religion nor rebellion is the answer, what's the explanation? In a nutshell, it's the Gospel. Pastor Tim Keller has articulated the Gospel in *The Meaning of Marriage:* "We are more flawed than we ever dared believe and more loved than we ever dared hope." While we don't have an acute answer to the "why" question in each specific tragedy, we have an ultimate answer.

It's interesting that Jesus didn't say *why* the tower fell; instead He chose to point us to a deeper answer—one that would last for eternity.

The Gospel writer Matthew quotes Jesus crying out from the Cross, "My God, my God, WHY have you forsaken me?" This is what makes the Christian God unique. We have a God Who knows what it's like to ask, "Why?" As much as we can tell, Jesus did not get an answer, but He loved anyway. He followed anyway. And so can you.

Recently, I had the privilege and pain of walking with a family through tough days. They lost their oldest daughter, age seventeen, in a car accident. She was days away from beginning her senior year of high school. A paradox occurs when two realities converge that don't make sense. In the New Testament, Paul writes about a paradox that occurs when believers lose someone they love: "We sorrow, but not as those without hope." I saw that paradox in this family who lost their daughter—incredible sorrow coupled with overwhelming hope.

In tragic moments such as these, people tend to slow down and think thoughts such as, "If something like that happened to me, am I ready?" or "I'd like for my life to count. I want to make a difference." When those same people voice those thoughts aloud, folks with good intentions will often say, "It's okay. Soon, you'll get back to normal."

If you ever find yourself thinking those thoughts, here is my encouragement for you:

## Day 17 Key Concept: Don't get back to normal

In those situations, you are actually thinking clearly. We *should* want our lives to count. We *should* desire to make an eternal difference. Don't get back to normal.

Jesus lived a morally pure life. Yet, He died an excruciatingly painful death that He didn't deserve. So, the religious answer won't work. Jesus proved that you can pursue God and love Him without having all of the answers. He loved and He followed, so the rebellious answer doesn't work. Jesus showed us that God is worth following—even when we don't have all of the answers.

## I'm New Here

One question newer believers have is, "What do I do when I'm mad about a tragedy or don't understand a situation?" Pray honestly. When you read the Psalms in the Bible, the authors pray honestly (yet not disrespectfully). They tell God how they feel. In some Psalms, such as Psalm 72, you see followers work out their belief as they pray.

_____

_____

_____

_____

_____

_____

_____

_____

_____

_____

_____

_____

_____

_____

_____

_____

_____

_____

_____

_____

_____

_____

_____

# DAY 18

## ON THE ROAD AGAIN

Sylvia is our youngest child. When she was four, her best friend Reagan had her first sleepover. Reagan had transitioned to a new bed and was going through the difficulty of staying in it consistently. So having our daughter over for Reagan's first sleepover was a "reward" from her parents. If Reagan could stay in her bed seven nights in a row, then Reagan and Sylvia could have the sleepover. Well, Reagan made it seven nights in a row. However, on the night of the sleepover, Reagan got up twice.

After her second appearance downstairs, her parents said, "You know, if you don't stay in your bed, Sylvia may have to go home." Reagan headed back upstairs, and Sylvia asked what happened. Unbeknownst to the two of them, Reagan's dad had snuck upstairs and listened to their conversation. Reagan detailed to Sylvia the impending doom if she could not stay in her bed. Sylvia—all four years of her—said, "Reagan, I am just your friend. I cannot help you solve this problem. You need to close your eyes, go to sleep, and wake up wiser."

Wisdom is so simple to give but so tough to live.

Wisdom is not just about knowledge, experience, and age. The Bible does say that gray hair is a "crown of wisdom," which for my family means we get "wise" at a very young age. I found my first gray hair as a senior in high school. When people see our wedding picture, they joke to my wife and me, "Who is that THAT?" My response is typically, "That's Angie and her first husband." But if your IQ, your age, and the degrees hanging on your wall don't make you wise, then what does?

Part of wisdom is seeing that your everyday decisions impact your future. Another way of saying that is:

## Day 18 Key Concept: Your road determines your reality

Good intentions are important, but your direction trumps your intention. You can't be going down *this* road and expect to end up at *that* destination. So wisdom is about getting on the right roads that point you in the right direction, leading you towards the right reality. The wisest man who ever lived says it this way:

**Proverbs 3:5-7a –** *Trust in the Lord with all your heart, and do not lean on your own understanding. In all your ways acknowledge him, and he will make straight your paths. Be not wise in your own eyes...*

I'm told that the Hebrew phrasing "do not lean" can also mean to "brace or support." In our vernacular, that would be like a crutch. Solomon is saying, "Don't trust your own understanding, especially the ones where you don't have expertise. However, where you do have expertise, just go with it on your own." I kid. I kid. That's NOT what Solomon is saying.

What Solomon says is that "in ALL of your ways" acknowledge the Lord or consider Him. Our trouble is the voice inside of our heads that says, "In this area, I'm smart enough, old enough, savvy enough, or experienced enough to handle this on my own." Additionally, our culture certainly doesn't encourage us to consider God before we make any decisions. The result is that we begin walking down our own road, headed in our own direction, and toward our own destination.

We can create some very curvy paths. Just ask anyone who's a little bit older than you. Curvy roads are generally harder to drive than straight roads. God is a Straight-path maker. Consider Him first.

Today, pray about the decisions you are approaching over the next twenty-four hours. Some may seem small. Some may be bigger choices you have to make. Where are today's decisions taking you on tomorrow's roads? Pray about how you can make choices today that will take you where you really hope to end up. If there are consistent patterns of bad choices in your life, then what if you talked to someone who you believe has Biblical wisdom? This makes having a local church family critical to following God.

## I'm New Here

When Solomon says, "Don't lean on your own understanding," it reminds me of the prevalent myth in our culture that Christianity is just a kind of crutch for weak-minded people. Besides the fact that brilliant scientists such as Galileo, Kepler, and Newton maintained a strong, Christian faith, Solomon is really saying we will all have a crutch. We will either lean on God's understanding, our own understanding, or someone else's understanding. Choose your crutch wisely.

_____
_____
_____
_____
_____
_____
_____
_____
_____
_____
_____
_____
_____
_____

# DAY 19
## FILLING IN THE BLANK

In Philippians 1, Paul makes an incredible statement that is both inspiring and confusing:

**Philippians 1:20-23** – *as it is my eager expectation and hope that I will not be at all ashamed, but that with full courage now as always Christ will be honored in my body, whether by life or by death. For to me to live is Christ, and to die is gain. If I am to live in the flesh, that means fruitful labor for me. Yet which I shall choose I cannot tell. I am hard pressed between the two. My desire is to depart and be with Christ, for that is far better.*

Paul wavers between the benefits of life and death. Yet, he was not thinking of *his* benefits, but about how his life could benefit *others*. He is torn between the two realities. As a pastor, I have the privilege of getting to know lots of people and have access to their lives. I often see people contemplate the reality of death. A few years ago, I met two men who left an indelible mark on me.

Every year in the United States, there are about six thousand diagnosed cases of a disease called Amyotrophic Lateral Sclerosis (ALS), also known as Lou Gehrig's disease. ALS attacks the nerve cells, which carry information from the brain to the muscles. So, there's a progressive loss of motor function. Out of three hundred million people, six thousand cases are diagnosed annually, which is two ten-thousandths of a percent (.00002).

I knew two men who were diagnosed with ALS in the same year within a month of each other—insane odds. I attended church with one of them, a man named Scott Shallcross. As crazy as it sounds, the other man is from my hometown; his name is Scott Bowling. I'll refer to them as Scott S. and Scott B.

Scott B. was an elected judge near my hometown and was coming to Columbus (the town where I live) for some training. As I was praying one morning, I sensed the Lord say to me, "Get the two Scotts together," so the meeting was arranged. On the day of their meet-up, Scott S. was having a tough day. For the first time, ALS had taken the motor function of his legs, and he was in bed.

When we arrived at Scott S.'s house, I introduced Scott to Scott. I watched them shake hands. Where they were once two physically strong men, this time their hands just met...no grip. This awful disease was slowly sapping their physical strength. They shared war stories about ALS and its effects on their bodies. Then, something I never would have expected happened.

Scott B., who's sitting beside the bed, says to the Scott S., who's lying in the bed, "You ever read Habakkuk?" Now, Habakkuk is a small book in the Bible that not many people can pronounce let alone read. Here's the conversation that followed:

Scott S. replied from the bed, "Nope."

Scott B. said, "You know what I love about that book? Habakkuk is one of those guys who asks God, 'Why?'" He looked at Scott S. and said, "You ever do that? You ever ask God, 'Why me? Why this horrible disease?' God told Habakkuk, 'It's going to get worse. I'm raising up the Chaldeans who will overthrow Israel.' Habakkuk says, 'God, why? God, how could you do that? The Chaldeans are the most evil people in the world. Why, God?'"

Scott S. asked, "What was God's answer?"

"God says, 'If I told you, you couldn't understand it, but can you trust me?'" Then Scott B. took out his iPad, held it with a withered hand, swiped to Habakkuk, and said, "Here's how the book ends."

**Habakkuk 3:17-19 –** *Though the fig tree should not blossom, nor fruit be on the vines, the produce of the olive fail and the fields yield no food, the flock be cut off from the fold and there be no herd in the stalls, yet I will rejoice in the LORD; I will take joy in the God of my salvation. GOD, the Lord, is my strength;*

*he makes my feet like the deer's; he makes me tread on my high places.*

After reading the verses, Scott B. said, "I told God…no matter what You do, I trust you. If you take away the olives and there's no cattle left, I'm going to believe You." Then, he said, "You know my feet are starting to give me trouble. And I sensed the Lord saying, 'Do you trust me with your feet? Do you trust me on the high places?'"

He continued, "I told the Lord, no matter what I trust you. This disease is my ticket to more of you, more of you if live or more of you if I die." Then he quoted Philippians 1:21 (the verse we read earlier), "For me to live is Christ and to die is gain. When God is all you have to live by, He's all you have to live for. I'm not afraid of death. I can't wait to see Jesus."

Scott S. quietly responded, "I know. I'm ready too."

That visit was one of the greatest privileges I've ever had as a pastor. Witnessing a believer take all of what God had given to him, the good and the bad, and view it as a way to know God more was incredible. And then, to see Scott B. use all of that experience to encourage Scott S. was a phenomenal testimony to God's power.

Today, as you take time to pray, I want you to fill in a blank:

## Day 19 Key Concept: For me to live is _____

For the Apostle Paul, life was not about avoiding death; life was about Christ. In the book *Heaven*, Randy Alcorn says that if you are a Christian, then this life is as close to Hell as you will ever get. However, if you are a not a Christian, then this life is as close to Heaven as you will get. Today, take the opportunity to thank God for the many blessings He has given you and write some of those blessings in the lines below.

## I'm New Here

As Christians, we need to fight entitlement. In Western culture, people tend to fight for their rights, some of which are real and some of which are assumed. We all have the tendency to get our privileges confused with our rights. One great way to fight entitlement is to regularly thank God for the good things He has given to you—especially the ones we take for granted.

_____

_____

_____

_____

_____

_____

_____

_____

_____

_____

_____

# DAY 20
## A BLESSED ADDICTION

When Paul writes to Galatian Christians in the New Testament, he communicates over and over again the meaning of Gospel—this idea that we are all sinful and messed up. However, God cleans us up through the work of Jesus on the Cross and through His resurrection. Maybe another way of communicating the first half of the Gospel is that we are all addicted to someone or something. I'll give you an example.

Nicolas Wig is from Minneapolis, Minnesota. James Woods is from St. Paul. Woods came home to find his cash, watch, and credit cards stolen. However, Woods also noticed Facebook was open on his computer and an account was pulled up—the account of Nicolas Wig. So, Woods messaged Wig telling him he was interested in buying a watch and asked for a meeting.

Wig showed up at the meeting the next day wearing James Woods' watch. Funnily enough, a few cruisers of Minneapolis' finest also showed up to take Wig into custody. How addicted to Facebook do you have to be to pull up your profile while you are burglarizing someone's house?!?!

We are all addicted to something: a drug, a drink, a boy or girl, a paycheck, or a promotion. Those are the obvious addictions. There are others: an abusive husband, a cheating wife, a dad who is never satisfied with your performance, or a mom who has been controlling your life well beyond adolescence. I have a friend who is over forty years old. He stands 6 feet 3 inches tall, and his mom still buys him size medium shirts like he used to wear in high school. In Scripture, Paul tries to convince the Galatians that we need a better addiction:

**Galatians 2:20 –** *I have been crucified with Christ. It is no longer I who live, but Christ who lives in me. And the life I now live in the flesh by faith in the Son of God, who loved me and gave himself for me.*

Paul is saying that, as believers, we have new lives. Another way of saying it could be:

## Day 20 Key Concept: Shelf your old self

Based on what Paul says, your old self can be crucified or put to death. Even more, we can have a new self that is empowered by God and that bears what Paul calls the fruit of the Spirit. Remember that we named the fruit of the Spirit earlier: love, joy, peace, patience, kindness, goodness, faithfulness, gentleness, and self-control. There's a rhythm, or a connectedness, to the fruit.

For instance, self-control is connected to joy. Our level of personal joy and contentment is not dependent on what we do possess or don't possess. So, we have self-control to the degree that we are content with whatever God brings into our lives. See the connection between joy and self-control? A lot of us have a version of self-control, but it comes from other places.

> Shelf your old self

I'll give you an example. Maybe the reason that the average (I emphasize "average") man doesn't show as much emotion as the average woman is because when men were young and cried, someone said, "Don't act like a girl."

So, little boys respond by drying it up. It gains you a measure of self-control, but only because men feel superior to women who may show more emotion. It's self-control born of arrogance instead of joy. Our tendency is to attempt to produce the fruit of the Spirit by our own strength. The tension the Galatians felt and that we feel are similar. Paul's critics said, "Your *works* make you *worthy.*" Paul enables us to see, "No. Jesus' work on the Cross makes you worthy."

Part of our daily prayer lives needs to be focused on giving God freedom in our hearts. When we enthrone Him, we dethrone any of God's rivals in our lives. Remember, the Father did not send Jesus to die on a Cross to give you a better version of your life. He died so you could have a brand-new life. Before you pray today, take a look at the fruit of the Spirit again. Which one(s) do you need the most help with right now? As you pray today, ask God to specifically begin the work of producing that fruit(s) by His power instead of trying to produce it through your effort.

## I'm New Here

The fruit of the Spirit is one of the most important basics of faith. John 15 says that Jesus is the Vine and we are the branches. As branches, we don't produce fruit. We bear fruit. Our work is to hang onto the Vine and allow Him to do the work in us—work that we cannot do in ourselves. That is why we want to make sure He is Lord of our hearts on a daily basis.

_____

_____

_____

_____

_____

_____

_____

_____

_____

_____

_____

# DAY 21

## LAND OF THE LOST

Recently, I was meeting some guys at Panera. At this particular Panera, the owners had installed some smoked mirror panels in the ordering area. After I ordered, I noticed a friend of mine, a pastor named Ryan, sitting on the other side of the panels—a perfect time for a prank. So I reached through the panels, put my hand right on the back of his head, and shoved hard just as he was about to take a bite of his panini.

It was really funny...until it wasn't. The man turned around, and I realized it was not Ryan. I looked at this guy whom I've never met (who now has some panini sauce on his cheek), and the only words that came out of my mouth were, "Wow, you're not who I thought you were." He looked at me and said, "Well, if it's any consolation, you're not who I thought you were." I apologized with a half dozen Cinnamon Crunch bagels and thankfully all was well!

Sometimes, we read the Bible and learn that God is not who we thought He was. We all have preconceived notions about God. Maybe you have heard from pop psychology about what God is like. Maybe a teacher, parent, or friend consistently asked a certain question about God that you were never able to answer. Genesis 3 expands our understanding of God and ourselves by revealing what happened in the Garden of Eden.

**Genesis 3:6-7** – *When the woman saw that the fruit of the tree was good for food and pleasing to the eye, and also desirable for gaining wisdom, she took some and ate it. She also gave some to her husband, who was with her, and he ate it. Then the eyes of both of them were opened, and they realized they were naked; so they sewed fig leaves together and made coverings for themselves. (NIV)*

Maybe the best way to describe Eden is that it was a world with thousands of "yeses" and only one "no." God asked Adam and Eve to obey Him about one tree. However, on one of their perfect days with their perfect lives in their perfect garden, Adam and Eve listened to the serpent's temptation. They bought into the lie that God was holding out on them, that there was better fruit.

They ate. And everything changed.

For the first time, maybe a lion looked at an antelope and raised an eyebrow. Maybe a shark smelled blood for the first time. Eve looked at Adam and thought, "You really ought to put some clothes on," so they found fig leaves. Then, they heard God coming. Sadly, for the first time, instead of running to greet Him, they ran and hid from Him. God asks perhaps the saddest question in the Bible: "Adam, where are you?"

Have you ever wondered why God asked that question? Does God know where Adam and Eve are? Yes. However, do Adam and Eve know where they now are? Not so much. Here's Adam's response to God's question:

**Genesis 3:10** – *He answered, "I heard you in the garden, and I was afraid because I was naked; so I hid." (NIV)*

In other words, Adam is saying, "Well, God, I was afraid because I was naked, so I hid." That response is a microcosm of human history when it comes to relating to God. In Eden, we see the beginning of fear, shame, and hiding.

We are afraid, afraid of trusting God's goodness just like Adam and Eve. Because of our fear, we try to make life work on our own, and we inevitably mess it up. You feel the weight of choosing the right spouse. Do you listen to the guidance that comes from a book like Proverbs or do you try to navigate the decision on your own? My wife was talking to a young mom who felt the weight of leading her family spiritually. She was leading alone. For whatever reason, she confessed, "I knew it when I married Clint. He had no interest in God. I even sensed it when I prayed. And I love Clint, but I should not have married him."

At some point, the reality of Adam and Eve's decision catches up with all of us. The rest of Genesis 3 tells the story of the consequences for Adam, Eve, and us. Causes have effects. For all of us, we struggle with sin from our earliest days. Parents don't have to teach their children how to take toys from other children. Kids will take a toy, look you straight in the eye, and say, "Mine," even when the toy clearly belongs to another child. Think about it: that's lying and petty theft—even before Kindergarten. It just comes naturally to all of us.

As well, God has an enemy who is always attempting to tempt us. It doesn't matter what time of day you turn on the QVC channel—they are selling something 24-7. Here's a watch that is also a toaster, and if you buy in the next ten minutes, you'll get a bonus set of wind chimes! Similarly, God's enemy is always trying to sell us on the reality that there's something better than God.

Here's the odd moment of Genesis 3:

**Genesis 3:21 –** *The Lord God made garments of skin for Adam and his wife and clothed them. (NIV)*

It seems God must have killed the first animal to cover Adam and Eve's nakedness. It brings up this idea:

## Day 21 Key Concept: Since Eden, God has been on a mission to cover our sins

You don't get three chapters into the Bible before you stop and say, "Wow, God, you're not who I thought you were!" The good news is that God knows exactly where we are and, more importantly, where we aren't in relation to Himself. Even more, God sent His only Son to die, so through His sacrifice on the Cross our sins could be covered. His death was a homicide of grace.

As you pray today, thank God again for the Cross. Thank Him that, even from the Garden of Eden, He had a plan to make a covering, an

> The death of Jesus was a homicide of grace

atonement, for your sin. Secondly, pray about the specific ways you struggle most with temptation. Adam and Eve struggled just like the rest of us. Ask God that He would both guard you from temptation and help you clearly see a way out when you are tempted.

## I'm New Here

When it comes to dealing with temptations, everyone is different. Some people tend to struggle more with walking on the wild side. Some tend to struggle more internally with things such as being judgmental. It's mission critical for us that we have a sense of our battles and pray those from the perspective of the Cross and Resurrection. Jesus gives us power to begin to overcome our weaknesses.

# DAY 22
## FEAR ITSELF

**Revelation 1:14 –** *The hairs of his head were white, like white wool, like snow. His eyes were like a flame of fire.*

Most people have questions about the Revelation, the last book of the Bible. The Apostle John was given a unique vision of Heavenly realities. I believe John did the best he could with the vocabulary he possessed to describe what he saw. In Revelation chapter one, he describes Jesus as having "eyes of fire." I believe this is a reminder to all of us that God sees everything. Nothing escapes His notice.

Moms have similar eyes. They somehow see everything all of the time. When I was a kid, my mom played the piano at our church. Even though she was keeping time with our small church choir, she still had the ability to see me all of the way in the back of the church. When I was making noise with my friends, I could feel the heat from her "eyes of fire" at the piano.

She would use those eyes to signal my dad, who would then bring that heat to my backside when necessary. As the congregation sang, "How Firm a Foundation" inside the church, MY foundation was getting a treatment by the old church bell. I earned it every time. Jesus' eyes see like that—completely and powerfully. How does that truth make a difference to us?

Since God sees everything, He knows everything. If He knows everything, we don't have to fear. A different way to say that is:

## Day 22 Key Concept: Don't let fear determine your fate

In multiple places in the Bible, God promises He will use even the worst situations and circumstances to shape us. Here's one example:

**Romans 8:28** – *And we know that in all things God works for the good of those who love him who have been called according to his purpose.*

As a freshman in high school, my son Dillon ran track for the first time. His team ran a guys/girls dual meet at Westerville Central, a large Division I school in the Metro Columbus area. The last event of every track meet is the 1600m relay (4x400) where every relay member runs one lap. The meet was running longer than scheduled, and it was getting late. Consequently, the officials decided to run the guys' and girls' relay teams in the same race. Dillon was running with a freshmen boys' team. The Westerville Central girls' varsity team was strong in the 1600m relay. You see where I'm headed here. Dillon ran the third leg of the relay. When he got the baton, the Westerville Central girls' varsity runner was right on my son's heels.

We didn't know the young lady who ran the third relay leg next to Dillon. We just know her first name was Tasha. Tasha was tall, and she had a stride like a gazelle. The reason we know her name is because all of her teammates were yelling, "You've got him, Tasha! Go get him!" Coming down the home stretch, Dillon left nothing in his tank and ran his best time by seven seconds.

After the race, my wife said to him, "You ran a great time!" He responded (still breathing heavily with his hands on his knees), "You can thank Tasha for that! I was just running down the home stretch saying to myself, 'I'm either beating Tasha or I'm not going to school tomorrow.'" There would have been no shame in losing to an athlete like her.

Tasha, wherever you are, you brought out the best and worst in my son. The worst is that the race was hard, but the best is that the win was good. We all have moments of difficulty in our lives. We all have times when it feels as if someone or something is relentlessly chasing us. Yet, God sees everything with His fiery eyes, and so we don't have to live in constant fear.

Fear is one of the most normal human emotions. However, it can become overwhelming. As you pray today, pray through your fears. What steps do you sense God wants you to take in your relationship with Him that fear is keeping you from taking? Maybe it's a relationship that needs reconciling, and God is encouraging you to take the first step. Maybe you have been falsely accused of something at work, and it will mean a confrontation. Don't let fear determine your fate.

> The race is hard, but the win is good

## I'm New Here

When I have the opportunity to talk with people about when they grew the most spiritually, they almost always say they grew the most during the difficult moments. I believe God would say to us, "I know the race is hard, but the win is going to be good." God does not waste anything that comes into our lives.

_____

_____

_____

_____

_____

_____

_____

_____

# DAY 23
## FREEDOM

Similar to many other countries, people in the U.S. tend to think of freedom in the context of political patriotism. Westerners think about freedom as a lack of limits. We rail against anyone telling us what we can and cannot do. This affects how we see life with God. The good news is that God wants freedom for us as well. Long before the Americas existed, God discussed spiritual freedom in the Bible.

**Galatians 5:13** – *For you were called to freedom, brothers. Only do not use your freedom as an opportunity for the flesh, but through love serve one another.*

As the Scriptures reveal, believers are called to live in freedom. However, freedom is NOT a lack of limits or boundaries. As a matter of fact, the opposite is true. Boundaries bring freedom.

Boundaries and borders clearly define a space or area. Typically, people find some measure of freedom within those boundaries. Humanly speaking, boundaries are necessary because choices have consequences. Consequences throw cold water on the idea that we have no limits in life.

In the verse above, Paul taught the Galatians that they were free to do whatever they want. Their problem (and ours as well) is that they were not clear about "whatever they want." Our hearts are full of conflicting desires. For example, say you want to eat nothing but Krispy Kreme donuts (especially when the "Hot Donuts Now" sign is on).

If you only eat Krispy Kremes, you are really, really happy—for a while. However, you don't want to be an unhealthy fifty-year-old with clogged arteries, so maybe you really aren't as free as you think. On the one hand, if you don't eat the Krispy Kremes, you have unfulfilled desire. This is a tragedy in the Western worldview. On the other hand, if you do eat the Krispy Kremes, you have to live with some guilt and fear. What does that scenario teach us about freedom?

## Day 23 Key Concept: Freedom isn't about doing whatever I truly want; it's about truly wanting whatever I do

Many of us attempt living on freedom's edge, occasionally crossing the lines. Just like Adam and Eve, we fear God may be somehow holding out on us. We imagine the fruit of one tree will somehow surpass the fruit of a thousand trees.

Of course, the danger is not the consequences, as we assume. The real danger is that we become two separate people: one who pretends to live inside of the lines and another who blurs the lines.

This kind of living has consequences, but interestingly, the consequences can actually become our friends.

A businessman traveled a lot for work and was sometimes gone for weeks. He thought he had every right to cross boundaries and break the covenants he had made to his wife and kids. He allowed himself privileges that he certainly wouldn't have given to his spouse. While at home, he was a model father, showing up at all of the football games and hockey practices. However, when he was out of town, he felt powerless to stop the "Mr. Hyde" who took over his persona. Sadly, this is not a fairy tale. I know this guy. We will call him Keith.

When Keith's wife learned about his out-of-town habits, he had to leave home. One evening, Keith had nowhere to stay, and he was too proud to reach out for help. All of the local hotels were booked because a large sporting event and a large concert were in town on the same night. So, this well-educated, well-rewarded business leader took a pillow and a blanket and slept in his car at a truck stop just off of a major highway.

He felt alone.

The next morning Keith woke to the sound of car doors closing. He could see other men walking into the truck stop. The irony is he was not alone at all. When he walked into the truck stop, the other men were getting coffee but saying nothing. This odd fraternity of men sleeping in their cars at the same truck stop knew nothing about each other, and yet they knew all they needed to know about each other.

As I processed this experience out loud with Keith, he was oddly grateful that his wife had found out about his second life. Instead of living two lives, he could now live one. The obviously painful side is that he had to deal with the consequences of his decisions. This began the hard work of trying to become one person, fully following Christ and living within his boundaries.

As you pray today, what are the boundaries and borders you struggle with the most when it comes to Christianity? Do you have anyone in your life who can help you navigate these choices? Pray for the courage to approach a godly, small group of people in a local church with whom you can connect. It may be a struggle with what you look at or how you spend your finances. It could be an addiction to food, shopping, or a chemical substance. God will walk with you to help you see what you truly want.

## I'm New Here

Finding a local church is not always easy. There are times when you show up the first day, and you just know the place will be your church family for a long time. Other times, you may have to visit multiple churches to find the right fit for you long term. Just remember, there are no perfect churches, just as there are no perfect people. Make

your preferences about a church's style secondary
to looking for healthy spiritual relationships.

_____

_____

_____

_____

_____

_____

_____

_____

_____

_____

_____

_____

_____

_____

_____

_____

_____

_____

_____

_____

_____

_____

# DAY 24

## THE SPIRIT IS WILLING

The Bible reiterates the importance of the Holy Spirit consistently. One conclusion we can clearly derive is that the Spirit always makes Jesus more real to us. The Holy Spirit does more than that in our lives, but never less. In one of the greatest chapters in the Bible, Paul answers two questions that the Spirit helps us with—two questions we don't even know we are asking all of the time. The first question is, "How can I know?" The second is, "How can I grow?"

A lot of us struggle with the question of assurance. How can I know for sure I'm a Christian? Perhaps you don't even know if you are a Christian or not. In Romans, Paul says the Holy Spirit gives believers spiritual life in the face of physical death.

**Romans 8:11 –** *If the Spirit of him who raised Jesus from the dead dwells in you, he who raised Christ Jesus from the dead will also give life to your mortal bodies through his Spirit who dwells in you.*

Because of Adam and Eve's sin in the Garden of Eden, we are born into the world physically alive but spiritually dead. This spiritual deadness means we are bent away from God, so we are spiritually separated from Him. In the above verse, Paul says that even though someday we'll all be physically dead, the Holy Spirit can make us spiritually alive through Christ. So, while physical death is inevitable, spiritual death is really up to us. One of my favorite pastors, Adrian Rogers, said, "For the Christian, physical death is a comma, not a period." When I say spiritual death, what I mean is we are all two people:

## There's a "bad" me and a "better" me

We all know someone who's worse than us, right? I may have done some bad things, but there's always Hitler to reassure my conscious, right? There is certainly a prodigal in all of us, but most of us choose the "better me" version of ourselves. We tend to justify ourselves with statements such as, "I'm not perfect, but...."

I was talking with a friend who lives in another city. He was expressing some confusion about Christianity, so I asked, "What do you think a Christian is?" He answered, "Man, I think being a Christian means you try to be a good person."

Now, here's a guy who has tons of biblical knowledge but still doesn't fully understand the heart of Christianity.

A lot of people would summarize Christianity that way. They would say something to this effect: "Being a Christian means that I'm going to attempt to be the most moral version of myself possible." Other times when I ask people, "Hey, when did you become a Christian?" they will respond, "Well, I've always been a Christian." However, as we saw in the verse from Romans, Paul contradicts both of those ideas.

Sometimes, it's harder for people who live out the "Better Me" version of themselves to find spiritual assurance. They think, "I'm good," but underneath they are really asking, "How do I know if I'm good enough?" The answer is proof.

In other words, is there evidence that you have turned away from self-reliance on your "Better Me" (your good works), and you have looked heavenward and said, "God, even on my best day, I'm not good enough to save myself. I need You to save me from my sin." After that kind of confession, you begin to trust Him to do the work you could never do in yourself—transformation. Then, the Holy Spirit begins His work of producing spiritual fruit in your life, which becomes the assurance of your salvation.

Even more, in Romans 8 Paul answers the second question, "How can I grow?"

**Romans 8:15-17 –** *For you did not receive the spirit of slavery to fall back into fear, but you have received the Spirit of adoption as sons, by whom we cry, "Abba!*

*Father!" The Spirit himself bears witness with our spirit that we are children of God, and if children, then heirs, heirs of God and fellow heirs with Christ, provided we suffer with him in order that we may also be glorified with him.*

Those verses are some of the most important in all of the New Testament. They mention the idea of being a son or daughter of God. Your big Bible word of the day is "sonship." Other verses, such as 2 Corinthians 6:18, also discuss how we become the sons and daughters of God. As a matter of fact, these verses say that all who are led by the Holy Spirit are, in fact, God's children. However, without the Holy Spirit, you're still a slave to your desires. Here's a way to summarize part of the Spirit's work:

## Day 24 Key Concept: The Spirit makes us sons instead of slaves

Some scholars suggest as much as one-third of the Roman world was slaves. The Roman world clearly would have understood the difference between living as a slave and living as a son. The average life expectancy of a slave was only twenty years, which meant there were many orphans who had very little hope.

However, Roman law said if a child was adopted, the child received full, equivalent privileges to the natural-born children of the adoptive family. That meant the adopted children would get an equivalent portion of the inheritance.

Paul says believers experience a similar, but better, adoption: "You have not received a spirit of slavery again to fear, but a spirit of adoption as sons whereby you cry 'Abba.'" In Paul's culture, "Abba" was the intimate word for "father." Today, we use the word "dad." The ability to cry out to God as Father reveals our relationship to Him. We aren't just His creation; we are His beloved children.

I have good friends, Matt and Kristy, who adopted their son Jeremiah from Ethiopia. He had a condition called "Food Insecurity," which is common to children who grow up in orphanages in other countries. Because these children haven't always had enough food, they want more than they should actually consume.

At age two, Jeremiah just wanted one more Nutri-Grain bar—all of the time. One night after having three Nutri-grain bars in the span of sixty minutes, Mom and Dad said, "No," and Jeremiah lay on the floor crying for one more bar. Kristy and Matt just wanted to open up the cabinet and say, "Look! Look how many Nutri-Grain bars we have for you. We love you. You are our son. You just can't have them all right now!" They were frustrated in a way only adoptive parents know.

Finally, Jeremiah went to sleep, and Matt and Kristy also headed to bed. Just before nodding off, Kristy sensed God saying to her, "Kristy, you're just like Jeremiah. You throw fits because you don't get what you want from me RIGHT NOW. You mope and whine when you don't get your way. Kristy, I'm your Heavenly Father, and you're my child. I love you. If you could just see into My cabinets…you can't imagine all that I have for you."

As you pray today, pray like a son or daughter of God. He's your Father. Pray from the perspective of His cabinets, His resources for your life. There's nothing He cannot do. Maybe His answer will be, "That's not best." Maybe His answer will be, "Not yet." Maybe today, His answer will be, "Yes." However, you can pray big prayers for your spouse, your kids, your co-workers, your family members, and yourself.

## I'm New Here

Praying long-term, vision-filled prayers is a tougher part of Christianity. We pray those kinds of prayers over years because we have hope. One of the fruits that the Holy Spirit produces in us is patience. Patience doesn't come through effort. It comes through reliance as we pray to see God's fruitful creation in our lives.

_____

_____

_____

_____

_____

_____

_____

_____

_____

_____

# DAY 25
## JUST UNDER THE SURFACE

Growing up in southern Ohio, I loved going to church. We went on Sunday morning, Sunday evening, and Wednesday evening—no questions asked. We had a deacon whose name was Bud. He stood at the door before most services and would give all of the kids a piece of this really cool, powdery pink candy as they entered. I would eat my candy, go to my pew, put my head in my mom's lap during the sermon, and sleep. It happened so often that one man at my church nicknamed me "Sleepy." Looking back, I wonder what was in that powdery pink candy.

Most folks at our church sat in the same seats. Gary and Imogene always sat in the pew in front of my mom and dad. On one Sunday, I didn't fall asleep for some reason. When I lay my head down, I could see Imogene's legs under the pew in front of me, and she had on sparkly hose. I became fascinated with those glittery hose because her legs were crossed and bent back under the pew right in front of me. The more and more I stared, the more and more the shimmering hose called out to me. I just had to reach out and touch her hose.

Imogene let out a loud, "Whew!" and I knew I had done something really wrong. The funny thing is that all of this happened below the pew, so no one could see my faux pas. Everyone else at our church thought she was having a moment of personal revival, and I'm certain the pastor thought he was on his A-game!

Unfortunately, there is a lot of stuff in our lives and in our churches that goes on just under the surface (or under the pew). Sometimes, most of the time, we pretend things are better than they really are. We all have the tendency to show more spiritual life than we really own. There was a couple like this in the Bible:

**Acts 5:1-2 –** *But a man named Ananias, with his wife Sapphira, sold a piece of property, and with his wife's knowledge he kept back for himself some of the proceeds and brought only a part of it and laid it at the apostles' feet.*

At the end of the previous chapter in Acts 4, a guy named Joseph sold a field and donated the proceeds to the church. The people rejoiced at his generosity, and I'm assuming his actions created some buzz around the church. In the beginning of Acts 5 (what we just read), a guy named Ananias and his wife, Sapphira, decide to do the same thing—except they didn't do the same thing.

They sold property and SAID they brought all of the proceeds. But in reality, they only brought part of the proceeds. Why would they do that?

## Day 25 Key Concept: It's impossible to escape the impostor in all of us

Pretending just comes naturally to all of us. I remember as a kid in the summer time, I'd open the curtain on the front window of our house around 3:00 p.m. I wanted to know just when my dad pulled up to the house after returning from the day shift at the steel factory. When I saw him pull up, I would quickly turn the TV off and pretend I was doing work or playing outside. That's the impostor—he's just in us.

> It's impossible to escape the impostor in all of us

We all tell stories where we are the hero, when we are really more of a coward. Famous coaches with very little to prove lie on their resumes. We pretend to be kinder, smarter, happier, prettier, stronger, and generally better than we really are.

There's a famous song in Americana about this phenomenon called "The Great Pretender." A group called The Platters sang it in the 1950s. The first verse says:

*Oh yes, I'm the great pretender*
*Pretending I'm doing well*
*My need is such I pretend too much*
*I'm lonely but no one can tell*

Ananias and Sapphira did not want to be generous as much as they wanted *to be seen* as generous. What's ironic about Ananias, Sapphira, and us is that people are always more drawn to the real you than they are to the fake you. As humans, we flock to authenticity because the desire for truth and reality is built into us. We bear God's image and His mark on our souls. However, we falsely think, "Our need is such," so we "pretend too much."

Maybe Ananias and Sapphira thought they deserved more recognition than they had received. We are that way at times. We think thoughts such as, "Doesn't anyone see how much I do? How much I accomplish?" Or we think, "How come no one notices how badly I'm hurting?" Subconsciously, we want to let everyone know, so we pretend that things are worse than they really are...we pretend too much.

Most of the time, we end up seeing pictures or a video from someone(s), somewhere in world, who is much worse off than us. This often helps us realize we need to cancel the invitations to our pity party.

As you pray today, pray for two different kinds of authenticity in your life. First, pray that God will consistently nudge your heart to pray truthfully. When something hurts, pray it. When you fear, pray it. When you are glad, pray it. Secondly, pray that God would give you the courage to seek out people, a few trusted people, with whom you can be transparent with in the difficult moments of life. As God brings those people to mind, both pray for them and write their names on lines below as way to remind you to look for those relational opportunities.

## I'm New Here

Pretending is an incredibly useless exercise, and yet so many of us struggle not to wear masks. First of all, try to remember God sees everyone and everything. Hiding from Him is hopeless. Secondly, if we clearly see this characteristic in others, then others will obviously see it in us. Finally, pretending limits the impact we can have for God's Kingdom in the long run. Strive to be appropriately authentic in a relational context.

_____

_____

_____

_____

_____

_____

_____

_____

_____

_____

_____

_____

_____

_____

_____

_____

_____

_____

# DAY 26
## I NEED A HERO

You are a five-star worshipper. You were created for it. Just look around and you will see people worshipping all of the time. I am an Ohio State football junkie. I say "The" Ohio State University. Just go to a game in the fall, and you will witness worship. Picture tailgating—people gathered in small groups around a common cause before the game even starts. They are eating together and talking to each other about the future of that day's win, sacrificing their financial resources, and singing with their hands raised. We are expert worshippers.

When our worship is God-directed, it becomes a long, endless conversation with Him. The more we focus in that direction, the bigger God gets. It's important for us to realize that our worship does not make God bigger. However, worship does increase our view of Him. And if we are going to consistently overcome fear, anxiety, and worry, it will take an ocean-sized vision of Him. If we are going to fight our anger well, we need to see a big God. If we are going to battle depression, a small God will not do for us. We need a hero. In the Revelation, we see a glimpse of Jesus, described as a Hero:

**Revelation 19:16 –** *On his robe and on his thigh, he has a name written, King of kings and Lord of lords.*

Here's the text definition of a hero: (a) someone who shows great courage or (b) the leader of a movement.

When it comes to dealing with our deepest flaws, you and I need a hero much bigger than our capacity. When I was in the seventh grade, there was a group of eighth-grade guys who ruled our school. They were the best athletes who dated the cutest girls, and their posse had a nickname—the Playboys. Their signature was that they all wore black Members Only jackets.

I was in the seventh-grade version of this gang, but I think we all wore white robes and were called the Choir Boys. Needless to say, the Playboys possessed a strong middle school intimidation factor. One night at a high school basketball game, I was in the restroom and in walked three Playboys. Now, I wasn't super popular with the Playboys because I liked one of the "bunnies" in elementary school.

My life flashed in front of me because when the Playboys fought, they fought together. While all of my seventh-grade friends were warming up their high tenor voices, I felt backed into a corner by three prizefighters. Suddenly, there was a noise—someone had entered the restroom—and, without hesitation, the Playboys dispersed. What happened? James Hall happened.

If Hulk Hogan and Xena the Warrior Princess had a child, it would have been James Hall...and he just happened to be my older sister's boyfriend. I like to think God touched James' bladder at that precise moment, so he would walk into the restroom and save me from my impending doom. When James entered the restroom, I suddenly had swagger (with a big dose of seventh-grade awkward) because I had a hero.

Now, we can try to deal with anger, for example, with our own strength. When we find ourselves getting upset and our temperature escalating, we can say to ourselves ten times, "I won't get angry; I won't get angry; I won't get angry." Most of us have tried a coping mechanism such as that with limited results. This is why we need a God Who is so much greater than our sufficiency.

Question: do you ever wonder why God demands for us to worship Him? Is He on some kind of an ego trip that He needs more people to worship Him? Here's the wonderful reality about worship:

## Day 26 Key Concept: We don't worship God because He needs it. We worship God because we need it.

As we worship, our view of God gets bigger. We invite His access into more of our lives. Yes, we are attracted to His power, but His love wins our hearts.

In 2015, I saw *The Force Awakens*, one of the *Star Wars* movies. In essence, the movie is a story about a father and a son. There's a moment when Han Solo finds his son, Kylo Ren. Ren is the Darth Vader (as a matter of fact Vader's grandson) of this movie. On a bridge with no weapon and no defense, Han Solo approaches his estranged son and asks him to come home.

I think Han Solo knows this reach, this love extended, will cost him his life. For his son to know "light," Han Solo has to face the darkness. For Kylo Ren to win, Han Solo has to lose.

We see the same picture of God in the person of Jesus. For us to win, Jesus had to lose—to die a painful, humiliating death on a Cross—for us to come home. Without Him, the Scriptures say we can do nothing that will pass the eternal test. We need Jesus, the original hero.

As you pray today, what are some things in your life that irritate you? Do you believe God is big enough to help you deal with anger? What things frustrate you over and over again? Are you trying deal with those things through your own suffi- ciency? Could you admit today to God that you need help? Ask Him for His capacity to deal with those irritations.

## I'm New Here

Anger is a two-sided coin in the Bible. In the New Testament, Paul tells the Ephesian Christians to "be angry and sin not." So, there must a kind of anger that is not wrong. The only logical, biblical understanding of that verse is that there will be times when you are angry at the sinful choices of others. You may find yourself upset because you see the coming consequences of those decisions for people you care about and love. Even in these dire situations, pray through them and live in God's sufficiency.

# DAY 27
## THE FILTER

A forty-two-year-old friend of mine developed arthritis in his hip, so at a fairly young age he had a hip replacement. He went to his first day of physical therapy, and his aggressive therapist put him through a battery of tests. After the testing, the therapist said to my friend (with a number of other patients in hearing range), "Jon, you are *impressively weak*. Your hamstring is weak, your glut is weak, your quads are weak, and your abs are weak. It's really quite remarkable." My buddy responded, "Thanks?"

To some, Jesus's death on the Cross makes Him appear to be weak. However, in one interaction with His Disciples, I believe He gave them (and us) the cure for ninety-percent of the dumb decisions we will make in this life, and this cure is tied up in the Cross:

**Mark 10:33-34 –** *"See, we are going up to Jerusalem, and the Son of Man will be delivered over to the chief priests and the scribes, and they will condemn him to death and deliver him over to the Gentiles. And they will mock him and spit on him, and flog him and kill him. And after three days he will rise."*

Jesus was not weak. He was impressively weak, and there's a huge difference between those two ideas.

This is the fifth time Jesus predicted his death to his Disciples. What should be becoming more and more apparent to them is that His death is not *accidental* to His mission but *central* to His mission. Christ's love is the greatest sacrifice. It's the nature of love. Parenting is a good example of this kind of love. I heard one of my favorite teachers, John Ortberg, once say this about being a parent:

> *You repeatedly read books that are boring to you. You have endless "why" conversations. Then, there's dressing, bathing, feeding, teaching them to do things for themselves. You do all of this to raise them, so that they can leave you just about the time they are beautiful and complete.*

However, some parents won't do it. They refuse to disrupt their lives that much; they refuse to give that much. As a result, their kids grow up physically but are still children emotionally. So, here's how it works: either the parents make the sacrifice or the kids make the sacrifice. Either the parents sacrifice temporarily or the kids sacrifice tragically. Somehow, the Disciples missed this point about sacrifice when Jesus was teaching them because a few verses later:

**Mark 10:35-37; 41** – *And James and John, the sons of Zebedee, came up to him and said to him, "Teacher, we want you to do for us whatever we ask of you." And he said to them, "What do you want me to do for you?" And they said to him, "Grant us to sit, one at your right hand and one at your left, in your glory."… And when the ten heard it, they began to be indignant at James and John.*

James and John were brothers. They came to Jesus and said, "Lord, we want you to do for us whatever we ask."

Here's a hint: maybe that's not the best way to begin a prayer. "Dear God, it's Dean. I'm here, and I want you to do whatever I ask you to. You good with that?"

The only thing worse than the brothers' opening remark was the request itself: "So, Jesus, when this Kingdom thing comes down, we want to sit on your right side and your left side." Now, at first this sounds as though James and John were simply saying, "Hey, you are the King, and we want to be senior Cabinet members," but it's more than that. They were asking to be the vice-presidents of the Kingdom.

Jesus responded with a series of questions: "You want to be on my right and on my left? Can you drink the cup (always a reference to God's anger against sin) I'll drink? Can you handle my baptism, my total immersion into the wrath of God against sin?" James and John replied, "Yep, we can." Similar to us, they were clueless about what they were really asking. And here is Jesus' reply:

**Mark 10:39-40** – *And Jesus said to them, "The cup that I drink you will drink, and with the baptism with which I am baptized, you will be baptized, but to sit at my right hand or at my left is not mine to grant, but it is for those for whom it has been prepared."*

The Disciples were thinking, "We're going to be royalty!" But Jesus was actually talking about humility. Following Him would not be glamorous; it would be painful; it would involve suffering. It would require humility. What did they miss? And what are we missing?

After Angie and I owned our first house for about eighteen months, Angie noticed we were struggling to keep our house clean. No matter how much we dusted, there always seemed to be a film on our furniture. So, I encouraged her to clean a little harder.

Total. Husband. Fail.

After mentioning it to my dad, he asked how long it had been since I changed the furnace filter. I replied, "There's a furnace filter?"

Just in case you don't know, here's how it works. Outside air is pulled into your house. On its way to visit the furnace or the AC unit, the air runs through a filter that removes outside dirt, pollen, dust, and so on. Then, the air goes into the ducts of your home, so you can breathe nice, clean seventy-degree air. The filter should be changed every four to six months.

Needless to say, the reason my wife could not keep the dust out was simply because her husband could not operate an AC unit properly. Here's what Jesus is trying to teach the Disciples:

## Day 27 Key Concept: <u>Humility</u> is life's <u>filter</u>

Let's define humility as us saying to God, "I need You." The opposite is pride, which is the idea that God needs us. Humility changes how we pray. As we begin to seek Him as our help, we pray things like, "God, I need you to change my spouse. I can't do that. God, I need you to change my relationship with my boss. God, I need you to change the dynamics with my extended family." Even more, your prayer should be, "God, I need you to change me."

Humility should *filter* everything in our lives. It should affect how we respond to everyone and everything. In other words, humility should clean the pride out. Just when we start thinking we are better than someone else, humility reminds us how flawed we really are. We should be impressively weak.

Today pray about those areas in your life where you sense that you need God to step in and you step back. Pray about your to-do list. You need Him for every item no matter how big or small. Let humility touch every aspect of today.

## I'm New Here

When you apply humility in the realm of relationships, you begin to pray differently. You are praying things like, "Please God, do what only You can do in changing them." You are also praying, "God, please keep changing me." You then gain an awareness of God's activity in that other person's life, as well as your own. You are putting your expectations on God and taking them off of the other person. The wonderful result is you decrease your dumb decisions where your relationships are concerned. Instead of trying to fix or manipulate others, you simply do your best to handle you and let God handle the rest.

_____

_____

_____

_____

_____

_____

_____

_____

_____

_____

_____

_____

_____

_____

_____

_____

_____

_____

# DAY 28
## CHALLENGES

I would guess most people have been challenged at some point in their lives. As a boy growing up in southern Ohio, a lot of our challenges seemed to involve fire. One Fourth of July, my friends and I got our hands on some Black Cat firecrackers. The idea was that we would light the firecracker and put it in our mouths as fast as we could, as if we were "smoking" them. The challenge, of course, was to see who could hold the firecracker there the longest. I never claimed we were smart.

I won! Sort of.

The Black Cat exploded about twelve inches from one side of my face. The good news was that the fire from the Black Cat ridded me of a developing unibrow. The bad news is that my ears rang for couple of days.

In the Bible, there is a famous fire challenge. For a period of about two hundred years after David was king, Israel had about twenty different kings. Each of these kings had significant character and leadership flaws, and each became progressively more evil. For example, about King Ahab, I Kings 16:29 says, "Ahab did more evil than all of the kings who were before him."

King Ahab enters a diplomatic alliance with the King of Sidon by marrying one of his daughters named Jezebel. Her name became synonymous with evil. When I was a kid, if you wanted to say a lady was mean, you called her a "Jezebel." Queen Jezebel pushed King Ahab to institute the worship of Sidon's gods, namely Baal, instead of the worship of Jehovah (Jehovah is a Hebrew name for God from the Old Testament).

Onto the scene comes Elijah, a prophet who spoke for God. Eventually, Elijah and King Ahab meet, and their meeting ends when Elijah says, "Let's have a challenge."

**1 Kings 18:21** – *And Elijah came near to all the people and said, "How long will you go limping between two different opinions? If the LORD is God, follow him; but if Baal, then follow him. And the people did not answer him a word."*

Elijah explains the problem very well for them and for us. He says to the people, "Look, there's no third option. If Jehovah is God, then follow Him. If Baal is god, then follow him. But you can't worship both." What's really relevant for us is that Elijah is pointing out there's not a legitimate third option. The reason the Hebrew people did not answer Elijah is they had monotheistic beliefs (a belief in only one God) and polytheistic behaviors (following the rituals of many false gods).

The false gods said, "If you worship me, I'll give you better crops. If you worship me, you'll have more kids." In other words, their idols were set up to give them a better, easier, happier life. Now, there's nothing inherently wrong with better crops or having more kids; those are certainly good things. But, we must remember:

## Day 28 Key Concept: Don't turn good things into god-things

Crops and kids make bad gods. If we are not careful, we ask our crops and kids to do for us what they were never designed to do—to fill our lives with joy. In doing so, we sabotage ourselves. The problem with false gods is that they promise what only the true God can provide.

In Western culture, money and beauty are maybe the most often worshipped false gods. Money says, "If you have enough of me, you'll be happy and secure." But how many people have plenty of money and find out they have cancer? Cancer doesn't discriminate. Money promises the peace that only the true God can provide.

We watch movies with attractive lead roles and are completely unaware that technology has "fixed" the actors' minor imperfections. Then we return to our homes and spend obsessive amounts of time analyzing our own physical imperfections. Our physical beauty will fade, but God can build a spiritual beauty in us worth an infinite, eternal value.

So, the question for us is, "Do we worship Jehovah on Sunday and money/beauty on Monday?" Just like the people in Elijah's story, today's

> False gods promise what only the true God provides

Christians have challenging moments in our lives when it comes to worshipping God alone. I have some international friends who described one these challenges to me.

Yusef, Bakta, and their families moved the U.S. from Nepal. They actually grew up in Bhutan, a country where there are very few Christians. Yusef said, "When I became a believer in Bhutan, I tried to share the Gospel. I went to the chief's home (similar to a mayor) in a village. I knelt down to show him Christ's humility. He hit me over the back with a chair. When I could get up, I looked at him and said, 'Jesus still loves you.' We left the village and claimed it for the Gospel. Eighteen months later, there are sixteen families worshipping together."

"The government eventually came to us and said, 'Either leave Christ or leave the country.' So, we went to live in a refugee camp in Nepal for eighteen years before coming here to the U.S." For some of us, our greatest challenge is what restaurant we are going to order take-out from tonight.

Looking back at Elijah's story, why doesn't God simply wipe out all of the people for worshipping false gods? Why doesn't God just wipe us out when we fail? The answer is Jesus. Instead of the Hebrews suffering and instead of us suffering for our failures, Jesus suffered in our place. He was our substitute who took the punishment we deserve. Instead of judgment, God offers us grace in the person Christ.

Spend some time praying today about your false gods. We all have different experiences, values, and perspectives. This means each of us will struggle in unique ways to see God as first in our lives. Ask God to show you what good things you are attempting to turn into god-things. Identify those, write them in the lines below, and pray them into their proper place in your heart.

## I'm New Here

Elijah teaches us that maintaining monotheism will not be easy. Western culture wants us to acknowledge that any and all gods are equal and legitimate. Christianity recognizes only one God. This truth means we have something to share with others. It does not give Christians a license to force people to act in certain ways or believe certain things, since we cannot change anyone. However, what we can do is tell our own story, which we discuss more in the next chapter.

_____

_____

_____

_____

# DAY 29
## STAY TO GO

Several years ago, I had to catch a flight early in the morning—a Monday morning. Traffic was worse than usual, so I had to sprint to the airport, where I then encountered longer than normal security lines. Fortunately, I made it through the security line quicker than I thought. So, I pushed my luck and hit Starbucks before heading to the gate.

I ordered an Americano and a blueberry muffin, which were delicious. But I was late heading to board the plane. With my hands full, I made it to the gate just in time. I noticed the first-class passengers standing there waiting to be boarded early. Now, I don't have anything against people who fly first-class. Or maybe I do.

Whenever I get onto a plane, I always feel as though the first-class passengers are eating their steaks from Ruth's Chris and having desserts from the Cheesecake Factory. They watch movies on their personal sixty-inch TVs, and I suspect they just wish I would get in my seat faster. I am sure none of that is really true…kind of.

While I waited to board that Monday morning with my hands full, a TSA agent walked by, made his way to the counter, and turned around rolling a carry-on bag. I thought, "Man, that looks exactly like my bag." Then, it dawned on me—that IS my bag. In my rush, I had left my carry-on at Starbucks.

The officer said in a loud voice, "Someone (which is code for 'Moron') forgot their bag at Starbucks!" All the first-class passengers must have been thinking, "Rookie." So, what did I do? I just had to lower myself, walk up there, and say, "That's my friend's bag; he's in the restroom. He's the moron." Just kidding. I couldn't do that because I'm a pastor, so I ate my humble pie in coach.

If we could, we would all probably edit out certain parts of our life story. Surprisingly, the most embarrassing and difficult parts of our lives are often the most attractive parts to others. Before Jesus left the earth and went back to Heaven, He "commissioned" His followers to share His story and their stories with the world. Here's how the New Testament book of Acts describes this message:

**Acts 1:8 –** *But you will receive power when the Holy Spirit comes on you; and you will be my witnesses in Jerusalem, and in all Judea and Samaria, and to the ends of the earth.*

Just a few verses earlier, Jesus had encouraged His followers to stay together in Jerusalem before they went out into the ends of the earth. While it's difficult to draw solid, long-term conclusions from those verses, some have recognized a pattern. Before we go out to speak *about* God, we must come in for fellowship *with* God. Another way of saying that is:

## Day 29 Key Concept: Ministry to the public is the result of my life with God in private

In other words, the natural result of my fellowship with God will be my desire to share spiritual life with others, to speak about God. Much like the early Christians in the book of Acts, this will look different for different people. God has wired all of us in unique ways. The ways we will hear God's voice, follow God's activity, and express His Kingdom to the world will most likely also be unique.

Among the unique, there is a constant. The constant is that we are all called to be part of God's Kingdom plan in some way. In the Bible, there are moments where God's Spirit moves in large, visible ways. There are also moments where God moves in smaller, much less visible ways. Our role is to work in concert with the Holy Spirit to help folks take steps towards God. Sometimes, we get to help them take a commitment step. Other times, we simply provide encouragement towards a larger step.

Sandy has been a part of our church family for over a decade. Shortly after getting to know her, she asked some people from our church to pray with her about her brother. He had been away from God for years. Then, she informed the group that she had been praying for her brother for over forty years.

When someone says that to you, a few assumptions immediately pop up. The first thing you tend to think is that if nothing has happened for forty years, the odds are pretty good that nothing is going to happen. The second sense you get is that someone is inviting you into more of a prayer marathon than a sprint.

That said, I remember the day Sandy shared with me that her brother had crossed the line of faith, after forty-two years of her praying for him. For over four decades, Sandy believed the best and prayed the best for her brother. She was able to talk with her brother about her faith and watch him take steps along the way towards his biggest step.

As you pray today, begin to ask God with whom does He want you to share the Gospel? Most of them will be people you already know such as family members, co-workers, schoolmates, and teammates. However, you should also pray about places that God might want you to become involved to serve the community. These opportunities will most likely be places with people you don't know as well. Where could God want you to connect with the world internationally? Maybe that begins with you praying for another country or people group. Make it a regular part of your prayer life to ask God for opportunities to help others take steps towards Him.

## In New Here

The whole idea of sharing our faith with others feels intimidating. Remember that Jesus didn't say for us to go "perfectly" to ends of the earth. Rather, we just need to go "willingly" to the ends of the earth. You don't have to know every answer. You can begin by sharing your story of what God has done in you. Then, rely on your local church to help you with more insight. Hopefully you will find a local church that has a desire to reach the nations, so you can be part of seeing the Gospel go to the ends of the earth.

_____

_____

_____

_____

_____

_____

_____

_____

_____

_____

_____

_____

_____

_____

_____

# DAY 30

## REMEMBERING

You've made it! Thirty days! I hope you are enjoying walking with God and that humility is filtering your life. I wanted to focus our last day together on the biblical concept of *remembering*.

As you get older, your brain has a way of recalling the important stuff and filtering out what's not so important, which is another way of saying you lose more of your memory the older you get. If you're old enough to be offended by that, don't worry.

You'll forget it in a few minutes.

Our youngest child has an uncanny memory for names. My wife couldn't think of someone's name because they had only met one time. However, our then six-year-old immediately recalled the name and said, "Mom, in our family, I am the great rememberer and you are the great forgeterer." When it comes to

God, we are sometimes great forgeterers. The Psalms remind us about our need to remember.

**Psalm 103:1-2 –** *Bless the* LORD*, O my soul, and all that is within me, bless his holy name! Bless the* LORD*, O my soul, and forget not all his benefits*

If you have made it this far into our thirty-day journey, you have exhibited a passion to walk with God. As we cross the finish line, I am going to share a few tools with you about developing your relationship with God. As you approach God each day, try to remember that He is your Heavenly Father. He wants to spend time with you. I try to remember that it's as easy as ABC.

## Asks

When you pray, you will have some requests, some "asks," each day. Some people feel guilty for making requests.

You shouldn't.

As a matter of fact, God commands us in the Bible to bring our requests to Him. Some of those will be for yourself. Some will hopefully be for others as well. Your asks will change over time as your prayers are answered. *Remembering* all God has done and "His benefits" are important. God can answer our prayers with a "Yes," a "No," or a "Wait." And sometimes, the asks will come from the second idea, the "B."

## Bible

I would suggest you pick a book from the Bible and read through it systematically. For example, start with John's Gospel in the New Testament. Read at least a paragraph each day. Don't stress about trying to get through a whole chapter of reading. Let God guide this time. As you read it, *remember* that this is God speaking to you. So, pray about WHAT you are reading AS you are reading. Here are some ideas to keep in mind as you read:

1. If the passage describes a sin you are struggling with, confess that sin back to God. Confession is powerful because it clears our relational path with God.
2. If the passage speaks about a command you need to obey, pray and ask for God's help to walk in obedience to that instruction.
3. If you read something in a paragraph to praise or thank God for, then pray the praise or thanksgiving as you are reading.
4. If you read a promise to us from Scripture, take time to pray and claim that promise.

*Remember*, your goal is daily, relational connectivity with God. You are not trying to read a certain amount each day. You are not trying to learn something new each day. Here's the "C."

## Calendar

I would encourage you to pray through your calendar each day. You know some of what is coming up in your day. Pray specifically for God to enable you to do what you cannot do on your own—make an eternal impact. Pray that God will help you see eternity in those simple, ordinary moments. Let humility filter your calendar.

At the same time, other everyday events happen that we never plan. Pray that God will both prepare you and use you in those instances as well. Pray for the people that you know you will encounter and ask God to use you to help them take steps towards Him. Then, pray that God will give you opportunities to impact people in the unexpected encounters as well.

Just think ABC.

In the end, Biblical remembering is not about mental recall. Instead, it's about what fuels you on a daily basis. Have you ever done something and said, "I'll never do that again"? However, within weeks, days, or maybe even hours, you find yourself doing that same thing again? It's not that you've forgotten, because you've got mental recall. It's just that over time you forget its effect on you. As the Psalms suggest, we are great "forgeterers."

## Day 30 Key Concept: We forget the things we should remember and remember the things we should forget

Spending relational time with God each day creates an environment for *remembering* in our lives. When we read His word and pray, we are reflecting on

God's purpose and activity in our lives. Without that time, we may hear a lot of truth, but it hangs out in the suburbs of our minds. Reflection drives God's truth downtown into our hearts.

When I met my wife, we were both in seminary. When we had classes together, I tried to casually sit next to her. When we had lunch, I found ways to nonchalantly (or maybe not so nonchalantly?) sit close to her. We also worked as interns at the same church, and I tried to find reasons to go near her office.

*Stalking* is way too strong of a word.

However, I wanted to put myself in her way as much as possible. Put yourself in God's way, as much as you can. Remember Him. Why would you invest so much time remembering Him? Because of how much He loves you.

Remember when Jesus was on the Cross, He cried out, "My God, my God, why have you *forsaken* me?" Jesus was forsaken as proof that you will never be forgotten. His death demonstrates that you will always be remembered by God. Here's what the Psalms have to say:

**Psalm 103:17 –** *But from everlasting to everlasting, the LORD's love is with those who fear him. (NIV)*

The ultimate Creator God, who stretched out the Heavens, had His only Son die on a cross and be forsaken for you. We need to remind ourselves regularly of the Gospel message. Become a great Gospel rememberer. Drive it downtown in your soul on a consistent basis.

Today, look back over the notes you have made throughout these thirty days. Which days were the most impactful to you? Why do you think those days left a mark on you? Take some time to pray and thank God for speaking to you in the last month. Don't let go of these truths. Find a local church and a solid small group within the church. Serve somewhere, share your story with others locally and globally, and live life with God each day.

Tomorrow, begin your prayer time by making your requests. Then, begin to read through a book of the Bible. If you don't know where to begin, start with the Gospel of John near the beginning of the New Testament. Read John 1:1-13. As you read, apply the questions that we discussed under the Bible section above. Take time to pray what you are reading, as you read. Then, take some time to pray through your day. You are ready to live everyday life with God.

## I'm New Here

I have a good friend who says, "What a man does once, he can do over and over again." What you have done for thirty days is the essence of Christianity. We have discussed some important truths: sharing your faith, serving your community, hearing God's voice, being part of a small group and a local church, and dealing with fear, anger, and loss. Remember, Christianity isn't about our being perfect; it's about our relationship with a perfect God. At any time, you can look back at the principles we have discussed. Take what you have learned and put it into practice—the practice of pursuing God each day.

_____

_____

_____

_____

_____

_____

_____

_____

_____

_____

_____

_____

_____

_____

_____

_____

_____

_____

_____

_____

_____

_____

_____

_____

# NOTES

1     Henry Blackaby, "Experiencing God: Knowing and Doing the Will of God," Lifeway Press, August 2007.

2     Wikipedia contributors, "Praetorian Guard," *Wikipedia, The Free Encyclopedia,* https://en.wikipedia.org/w/index.php?title=Praetorian_Guard&oldid=797514569 (accessed September 2, 2017).

3     Steven Greenhouse, "Americans' International Lead in Hours Worked Grew in 90's, Report Shows," (*New York Times*) Sept. 1, 2001.

# ACKNOWLEDGMENTS

The Father, Son, and Spirit who have made me a son, an heir, and a part of the Kingdom Body.

Angie – thanks for the time away during Sabbatical 2017 to write. I'm grateful for a love that gets stronger, as it gets older.

Sydney, Dillon, and Sylvia – you make it fun to be a dad!

Allison Myers – thanks for your countless hours of editing and encouraging a first-time author. You have an incredible gift.

Kary Oberbrunner – I remember the day you said to me, "You should write this book." I appreciate your friendship and encouragement along the way.

Shane Tucker – thanks so much for the great cover design work (shanetucker.com)

Parents – Dad and Mom, the sacrifices you have made for me are too many to tell. I'm grateful for every one of them.

Mentors – if I named one specifically, I would leave too many out. I am grateful to stand on your spiritual shoulders.

Lifepoint Staff – there is no other leader that is more supported than me. You bless me over and over again with the way you desire to see the world changed.

Lifepoint Church – being your Lead Pastor is a privilege, not a job. I wish every pastor could serve with a people like you.

Please connect with Dean at deanfulks.com

or check out more resources at:

www.lifepointohio.com